Know Well (Wealth) Your Flocks and Herds

Know your finances and get out of debt

TBANKS

Copyright © 2020 TBanks.

All rights reserved. No part of this book may be used or reproduced by any means, graphic, electronic, or mechanical, including photocopying, recording, taping or by any information storage retrieval system without the written permission of the author except in the case of brief quotations embodied in critical articles and reviews.

This book is a work of non-fiction. Unless otherwise noted, the author and the publisher make no explicit guarantees as to the accuracy of the information contained in this book and in some cases, names of people and places have been altered to protect their privacy.

The information, ideas, and suggestions in this book are not intended to render professional advice. Before following any suggestions contained in this book, you should consult your personal accountant or other financial advisor. Neither the author nor the publisher shall be liable or responsible for any loss or damage allegedly arising as a consequence of your use or application of any information or suggestions in this book.

WestBow Press books may be ordered through booksellers or by contacting:

WestBow Press
A Division of Thomas Nelson & Zondervan
1663 Liberty Drive
Bloomington, IN 47403
www.westbowpress.com
1 (866) 928-1240

Because of the dynamic nature of the Internet, any web addresses or links contained in this book may have changed since publication and may no longer be valid. The views expressed in this work are solely those of the author and do not necessarily reflect the views of the publisher, and the publisher hereby disclaims any responsibility for them.

Any people depicted in stock imagery provided by Getty Images are models, and such images are being used for illustrative purposes only. Certain stock imagery © Getty Images.

Editor: Deanna Banks

ISBN: 978-1-9736-8279-0 (sc)
ISBN: 978-1-9736-8281-3 (hc)
ISBN: 978-1-9736-8280-6 (e)

Library of Congress Control Number: 2019920856

Print information available on the last page.

WestBow Press rev. date: 07/13/2020

NIV: Scripture quotations marked (NIV) are taken from the Holy Bible, New International Version®, NIV®. Copyright © 1973, 1978, 1984, 2011 by Biblica, Inc.™ Used by permission of Zondervan. All rights reserved worldwide. www.zondervan.com The "NIV" and "New International Version" are trademarks registered in the United States Patent and Trademark Office by Biblica, Inc.™

RSV: Scripture quotations are from Revised Standard Version of the Bible, copyright © 1946, 1952, and 1971 National Council of the Churches of Christ in the United States of America. Used by permission. All rights reserved worldwide.

KJV: Scripture taken from the King James Version of the Bible.

CEV: Scripture quotations marked (CEV) are from the Contemporary English Version Copyright © 1991, 1992, 1995 by American Bible Society, Used by Permission.

NKJV: Scripture taken from the New King James Version®. Copyright © 1982 by Thomas Nelson. Used by permission. All rights reserved.

MSG: Scripture quotations marked MSG are taken from THE MESSAGE, copyright © 1993, 2002, 2018 by Eugene H. Peterson. Used by permission of NavPress. All rights reserved. Represented by Tyndale House Publishers, Inc.

NASB: Scripture quotations taken from the New American Standard Bible® (NASB), Copyright © 1960, 1962, 1963, 1968, 1971, 1972, 1973, 1975, 1977, 1995 by The Lockman Foundation Used by permission. www.Lockman.org

AMP: Scripture quotations taken from the Amplified® Bible (AMP), Copyright © 2015 by The Lockman Foundation Used by permission. www.Lockman.org

AMPC: Scripture quotations taken from the Amplified® Bible (AMPC), Copyright © 1954, 1958, 1962, 1964, 1965, 1987 by The Lockman Foundation Used by permission. www.Lockman.org

HCSB: Scripture quotations marked HCSB are taken from the Holman Christian Standard Bible®, Used by Permission HCSB ©1999,2000,2002,2003,2009 Holman Bible Publishers. Holman Christian Standard Bible®, Holman CSB®, and HCSB® are federally registered trademarks of Holman Bible Publishers.

ERV: Taken from the HOLY BIBLE: EASY-TO-READ VERSION © 2001 by World Bible Translation Center, Inc. and used by permission.

GNT: Scripture taken from the Good News Translation in Today's English Version- Second Edition Copyright © 1992 by American Bible Society. Used by Permission.

Thanks

My Lord and God, Jesus Christ, who inspired a non-writer like me, to write. He does have a sense of humor. Thank you much, love you more.

To my wonderful wife, Lowanna, who supported my efforts in writing this book. She provided her insight and wisdom from our financial experiences. To our children, Larone, Tia and Larren, for being a part of our financial transfiguration. To my mother, Ruth(D) and siblings, Richard(D), Glenn(D), Lillian, William, Gregg and Joe, for allowing me to share some of our childhood stories. To our Pastor and home church for allowing myself and my wife to grow a financial ministry. And to the Department of Defense for telling me for 28 years that I could not write.

To Dave Ramsey's 'Money Makeover' and the Financial Peace University (FPU) class, which started us on the road to transfiguration. We read the book in 2006 and took the class in 2008 at a co-worker's church. In 2009, we became Dave Ramsey's Financial Peace University (FPU) Coordinators at our church and have initiated 22 classes since.

Thanks Dave.

CONTENTS

Foreword xi
Introduction xiii

Got Poor? 1
Got Debt? 15
Know Your Flocks and Your Herds 29
Now You Know – Ruminato 44
Frugal 56
Time To Go 65
What To Do/How We Did It 72
Stewardship 91
Prosperity 116
Giving 131

Consultation Stories 151
Additional Scriptures 161
Notes 163
Household Budget 167
Rapid Debt Repay 169

Foreword

Ted Banks and Wealth Knowledge have been holding hands for a long time. They have walked in unison through good and bad times. There have been blessings, and there have been depressions. Through it all, Ted has kept a strong heart and positive mind set in his journey.

To know the author, whom I have been privileged to know for fifteen years, one understands that defeat is not in his resume. He is a total winner with a triumphant pace in his walk. I love the man as a brother. The Bible says a friend loves at all times, but a brother is born for adversity.

Ted is a wonderful friend and an amazing brother.

When you read his story of Money and Wealth management, you will pick up his heartbeat as a normal man that had an "out of this world" plan!

I am so happy to introduce *Know Well (Wealth) Your Flocks and Herds* to you.

You will smile and laugh while ingesting this read. However, you will begin to see his unusual view in the process of how to make and manage money.

I recommend this great read. If you ever get an opportunity to meet the author, please take advantage of that because the man is better than the book!

Rex Johnson
Senior Pastor
Christian Life Austin

INTRODUCTION

It was a typical Tuesday morning which normally found me reading a chapter out of the book of Proverbs. It was the 27th day of the month. I only know because I was reading in the 27th Chapter of Proverbs, trying to keep my goal to read that certain chapter on that corresponding day. I normally do my three "S's;" sit, shave (electronically) and study (my Bible). I normally read in the early hours prior to going to work. At the time, my wife and I were the coordinators of a financial class at the church we attended in Austin, Texas. While I read, I would write down scriptures pertaining to finances to use in that class. There are enough scriptures about money in the book of Proverbs to obtain some kind of financial degree. Most of the verses provided knowledge and wisdom regarding spiritual life, relationship and prosperity. From do's to don'ts, from woulds to wonts, the book of Proverbs can be thought of as both a spiritual and a financial guide. After many scriptures on what to do and what not to do with your money (which is not really your money, but I won't go there now, because I want you to finish the book), God opened-up my understanding to a verse which I had read many times before. The scripture did not tell me what I needed to do about our finances or how I should go about it, but rather what I should know about our finances. I felt that God was sharing with me, that before I should do what I needed to do, I should "know" what I needed to "know."

I was so impressed and so motivated by what God was impressing upon me, I was moved to do something. Now I am not trying to scare away the meek and mild who can't handle the fact that there is spirituality in their finances. I was so excited, I went to my wife and said, "look at this scripture, I think God wants me to write a book." She, not as excited, said something like, "that's good honey." All the while she was probably thinking, "what about that tear in the carpet I asked him to fix 3 months ago, or that planter I asked him to make me last year, or the other 6 million other things on the Honey do List." Well maybe she didn't think 6 million, but I understood her response. Look, I am that guy, who for 20 years with the Federal Government, couldn't write an investigative report without my supervisor bleeding red ink all over it. If I had really been smart, I should have invested in the "Red Ink Pen Company" when I started with the government. I know, I would have never wanted me to write this book. And I know that the devil did not want me to write this book. Now ten years after that Tuesday morning, I am getting this book published. No, I did not write a sentence a day. I wrote this book and rewrote it. I edited and re-edited. One thing I have come to realize in my relationship with God is that everything is done in his timing. Even the publishing of this book.

I wrote this book for two reasons; 1. to help those who have become so frustrated with their financial situation because they do not know where to start. 2. Obedience to God. It is my hope that this book would encourage someone to do something about their finances and/or that it would contain an answer to help someone free themselves of their financial bondage. Christ came to set us free, from all bondage, debt is a bondage.

Thank God and thank you.

Got Poor?

Broke is a temporary condition, poor is a state of mind....
"Poverty and The Poor" quote by Sir Richard Francis Burton

As a child, I thought we lived in the state of Texas, but I see according to Sir Richard Burton, we must have lived in the state of Mind, where ever that was. When I was five years old, my father left my mother with seven children. Up until that time, the rural house we lived in had lights, but not much more. No phone, no water, no plumbing, no bathroom, not a single luxury. It was almost like Gilligan's Island. We didn't have a broken-down boat, but we did have a TV. We left that house and moved into the city where most of the houses we lived in only had cold water and electricity. We thought we were doing alright. I knew we lived in a state of need, but I didn't know we lived in the state of poverty. I guess because we were "too-po, too-kno," the status of our condition. Unlike the condition where you know you're poor and you focus on that. I didn't find out how poor we were growing up until I went to a big liberal university. The courses I took let me know how much of a poverty-stricken environment I had been raised in. Our mother however, kept us from focusing on our environment by loving us and making us be responsible for our actions in life. Plus, poverty was not an issue to me because most of our neighbors only had a little more than us. I thought we were alright.

Living in the city in the early 1960's, provided more opportunities for a kid like me and my peeps to make more money than when I lived in the rural country. We sold soda-water (pop) cans and bottles, stole (I mean found) copper wiring from empty homes and sold it to Bully Grays Salvage yard (I believe the stature of limitation has expired). Bully Grays was an interesting place, although an established salvage yard, his place was also a repair shop and a day-old pastry store. After getting our hard-earned lucre, we often purchased some of Bully Grays day or five- day old pastries, Hostess Fried Fruit Pies. Hostess cherry pie was my favorite. A pie was worth about 10 aluminum soda cans, even if it had some mold on it. That was ok, he gave exchanges. One summer, my brother and I and our friends decided to make a lot of money by picking cotton. The job paid 2 cents for every pound of cotton we picked. I worked hard the first few days, then it became a fun fest in the cotton fields with me and my friends. I think I made about $15. Wow, I thought I was rich. It was the most money I had ever had in my life. When I got home, I showed my mother the money I had made. She asked to borrow the money. That was the last time I saw that great fortune. I never asked my mother about the money. As a ten-year old, I somehow sensed or knew that mom needed the money for the family. People who support the hiring of illegal immigrants say Americans won't work certain jobs, I'm not buying it. American's won't work certain jobs as long as they can sit at home and get money from the government for doing nothing. Growing up without money taught me that I could work any job that paid enough for me to eat.

In the state of Texas in the 1960's, it was difficult for single black mothers to obtain public support for their children. In our case of seven children, there definitely wasn't enough support to live on. So, we moved to Columbus, Ohio. There is a Christopher Columbus Monument at City Hall in downtown Columbus which was saying to me "'Give me your tired, your poor, your huddled masses yearning to be free." I'm sorry, wrong statue. Actually, he represented a better place to be where we could get more welfare. We now lived in the city where Aid to Dependent Children (ADC) was alive and flourishing. Another antipoverty social program was Model Cities. Model Cities was designed to lift people out of distressing, degrading and oppressive conditions. Before experiencing the Model Cities, we lived with our uncle for a short period of time on the southside of town. It was a nice racially mixed neighborhood with moderately priced homes. It was a very nice house for black folks. After several weeks, our mother rented a home on the East side of the city. Now I know why some cities have east sides, that's where the misfortune goes to live. It's a good thing that at that time I hadn't heard of the scripture *"Misfortune pursues sinners, but prosperity is the reward of the righteous"* (Proverbs 13:21 (New International Version (NIV)). I would have thought we were sinners. Oh yeah, we all are sinners. Thank Jesus for those saved by His Grace.

    I remember the first day we moved into our east side home. It was a big five bedroom, two bath, double brick home. Poor? I thought we were rich. I mean compared to the shack we lived in in Texas - a two bed room, cold water bath room, wooden structure, which had no stud walls and the only insulation the house had was its wall paper which kept the wind from freely blowing through the house. I have often commented that I could look through a crack on our front porch and see completely through the house to our back yard, without looking through a door or window. One space heater and the gas stove were not enough to warm the Texas house, even after we stuffed clothes and cardboard into the broken and missing window panes. In the summer, mosquitoes freely entered through our air-conditioned windows, sucked our blood and left saying "We'll be back for more withdrawals." The house in Columbus was brick with real walls and panes in every window. There were a lot of windows, stairs to the second and third floors, floor registers that provided heat, a basement, which was used as our indoor football field, and a detached garage. Move over George Jefferson, we had moved up to the east side. I often thought if we had that house in Texas, we would be considered rich. Did I mention the house was a double and it came fully equipped with another family next door? Two houses stuck together to make one, I did have some things to learn in life.

One of the things I quickly learned about was the welfare system. I learned that on welfare, the more children you had, the more help you got. A river of milk, dozens of eggs, stoppem-up cheese and Sam's sand-paper cereal, and food stamps. Don't get me wrong, to a hungry child those items proved to be very filling. I was thankful for the help, in fact very thankful. However, my experience with the welfare system was embarrassing and degrading to my esteem. I can recall the fear and shame of having a classmate seeing me at a local grocery store buying food with food stamps. On more than one occasion I ran into a classmate in a grocery store and to keep from being embarrassed, I would take my items off of the checkout counter, get out of line, and pay for them later after the classmate had left the store. It was an embarrassment to me being on welfare. There was nothing more embarrassing than to have your classmate at school call you out in front of the class and say, "didn't I see you with food stamps?" My classmates in junior high school at times were brutal. Many of them looked for evidence of poor-welfare children so they could shame and belittle them. A faith-based organization named Charity Newsies of Columbus, provided "needy" children with distinct and identifiable clothing. I remember the first time we wore those clothes to school and the kids ridiculed us so badly, they literally chased us home calling us "needy," "Charity Newsies," and "welfare kids." Yeah, that is what we had become; poor, needy, welfare kids. It was cruel, hurtful, embarrassing, dehumanizing and all those other adjectives that say you are worthless. Even today, remembering those days brings tears to my eyes. I saw so many young people who accepted this lifestyle and developed little interest in bettering themselves. The only way I knew to better myself was to go to school and get a job. Unfortunately, some had an attitude of "why work when you don't have to," in fact, "why even go to school?"

While I am talking about schools, let me give my observation of how schools (in Texas and Ohio), affected my mental wealth development. For example, the junior high school I attended in Texas was small, poor and black. I can't remember one white person at that school, not even a lost one looking for directions. At that time in the south where separate but equal (in theory) was mostly the way of life, blacks went to black schools, whites went to white schools and browns went to what was left over schools. I apologize if these terms offend anyone. You see, blacks were black before they were African American, whites were white before they were Anglo/Euro Americans and browns were browns before they were Mexican Americans. We spend more time and money labeling people than we do helping them or their situation. Sorry, I digress. When I went to school in Ohio, I attended a large, poorly controlled, black junior high school. Unlike Texas, there were several white students, maybe two and plenty of white teachers, well more than two. I was at best a "C" student in Texas, but in Ohio, I was an almost-straight "A" student. Not because I had an epiphany of knowledge, or drank a potion from a nutty professor, or paid some teacher off (remember-no money). The difference was my mediocre work efforts in Texas netted me a "C" grade, however the same mediocre work efforts in Ohio netted me an "A" grade. In Texas, we did not have much, but one thing we did have was respect for the school and it's teachers. If we disrespected our teachers, we had to meet the board and I don't mean a member of the Board of Education. I mean the board of correction (pain). I know some of you are horrifyingly saying "No!," to corporal punishment. Well you should say, "yes," it might just straighten out a few of those attitudes you really dislike in your little darlings. My mother had seven children to raise. She did not have time to deal with attitudes and disobedience. And if she got word from a school official that one of us were acting inappropriately, we got our butts beat. *"He who spares the rod hates his son, but he who loves him is careful to discipline him"* (Proverbs 13:24 NIV). At that junior high in Ohio, someone tried to burn the school with a Molotov cocktail. The American flag was set on fire and a student shoved a teacher, trying to provoke a fight. All of this was on my first day at that school. I think the teachers appreciated my efforts, even though mediocre, and the respect I showed them. *"He who scorns instruction will pay for it, but he who respects a command is rewarded," (Proverbs 13:13 NIV)*. I am not even sure I deserved all those A's, but I'll keep them anyway.

God's financial principles, since this is a financial book, are not just for grown-up folks, but for young folks too. The earlier we can apply them to our lives or the lives of our children, the better off we and they will be. While attending the school in Ohio, I noticed how well dressed many of the kids were. I knew that most of those kids were from single parent homes like mine and were on welfare. How they were affording designer jeans and $100 Nike tennis shoes was beyond me. They looked rich but, in reality, the economic scale indicated that they were poor. *"One man pretends to be rich, yet has nothing; another pretends to be poor, yet has great wealth"* (Proverbs 13:7 NIV). These same kids grew up and bought luxury cars they couldn't afford and acquired debt they could not render, but they looked good pretending to be rich. I never pretended to be poor, but I was told I was poor. In fact, I was so poor, I couldn't even afford to pretend to be rich.

If this transformation from one state to another affected me and my siblings, imagine how it affected our mother's life. The state's assistance was a help, but wasn't enough to live on. My older siblings got jobs to help the family. The assistance we received from the welfare department would have been reduced if my mother worked a legitimate job. Our mother would find work where she could get paid in cash, under the table. That cash was untraceable by the welfare department and our assistance not reduced. So, she found work at a bar on Main street on the East side of town where she was paid in cash. She worked long hours for little pay. I believe she made more money off her tips than from her actual pay. We lived a few miles from the bar and mom did not have a car. She often depended on friends to give her a ride or she would walk. Mom got me a job at the bar, sweeping, picking-up and cleaning the outside. I worked after school five days a week and it took me about 30 minutes to sweep the side walk and pick up all the beer bottles and cans. The job paid five dollars a week. One whole dollar a day. One evening, I was picking up at the bar and inadvertently startled a man who attempted to pull his gun on me. He had been drinking and had a difficult time getting the gun out of his pocket. I started to think my life was worth more than a dollar a day, so I asked for a raise to ten dollars a week. That following Friday evening, when I finished my work, I went to collect my five dollars from my mom, who normally paid me. She paid me ten dollars. Now that's what I was talking about. The "Man" (the owner of the bar) saw my value. The owner of the bar was a Jewish man. Not that it makes a difference, but since I have mentioned other ethnicities, I might as well throw the Jews in here also. I thought I had gained a victory for the underpaid workers who risk their lives for their jobs. After paying me, then, my mom told me that the owner said I was fired because he could not pay the increase. For my mom to tell me that, it hurt a little, but it was also a small relief. It was not worth it for me to ride my bike or walk to that job daily for a dollar. Once again, I was thankful to have a job, but like God does, he closes one door to only have another one open. Shortly after that, I got a part-time job working at a grocery store on Main Street, next to a bar, which was worse than the bar where I had been fired. At this bar, people were stabbed or shot weekly. I worked part time and made about twenty-five dollars a week. Ching-ching! I guess my life was worth more there.

To all those good hearted, well meaning, liberals, I want to say thank you. Thank you for giving me a taste of your socialistic programs which told me how victimized and poor I was. You started me on the road to conservatism. According to an article, "The Effects of Poverty on Education in the United States," by the Childfund International, "Children from lower-income families are more likely than students from wealthier backgrounds to have lower test scores, and they are at higher risk of dropping out of school. Those who complete high school are less likely to attend college than students from higher-income families. For some children, the effects of poverty on education present unique challenges in breaking the cycle of generational poverty and reduce their chances of leading rewarding, productive lives." Family generational poverty indicates that a family has lived in poverty for several generations. That means our family must be in generational poverty to the tenth power. These generational poverty conditions might be facts by the Childfund International, but certainly it is not truth. For the Bible says in Matthew 19:26(NIV), *"Jesus looked at them and said, With man this is impossible, but with God all things are possible."* It is possible that a Cesar Chavez, a Ben Carson or a (your name) can overcome poverty and excel beyond the facts of the Childfund International. My wife and I, through Christ, broke the generational poverty curse, because with Christ, all things are possible.

Know Well (Wealth) Your Flocks and Herds

For a country kid from Texas, I found the North to be cold, both climate wise and emotionally. People just didn't seem truly friendly or sincere. I was threatened with physical violence at school and on the play grounds. I was approached by drug dealers, homosexuals and even pressured for sex. The people on the east side of Columbus were economically better off than we had been in Texas, but many were morally bankrupt. The neighbors we had were decent people. Like most people, just surviving on the lower socio-economic ladder of society. Just next door to us was a family, which had several young ladies. Like our family, there was not a father in their home. One of the young ladies eventually became my wife. Our relationship was not one of love at first sight. When I first met my wife, she was in the 8th grade and I was in the 9th grade in junior high school. We lived in duplexes next door to each other. I first saw her with some of the other girls in the neighborhood, talking in their front yards. Like I said, it was not love at first sight, it was cordial. Over the next three years, we became friends. I found her to be nice, pretty and virtuous. She also talked very fast for my slow Texan ears, the way many Northerners talked. It took me about a week to learn her name because she spoke so fast. She hurt my feeling at first with some of the things she said about me being from Texas. Of course, she had to say it three times for me to understand her. I was 14 years old when we moved to the east side, 10 years later I married my wife.

Let me say this about socio-economic status of my wife's family. They received subsidized housing and food stamps. Her mother received some type of community training, a part-time job and eventually obtained a position with the State of Ohio. As she moved up the financial ladder and made more money, her benefits were reduced. After several months of working with the state, her benefits were terminated. I asked my wife if she had considered her family poor, during the years they were receiving welfare. She said she was not aware that they were poor until someone told her that she lived in the "Model Cities." The Model Cities was an antipoverty program started in the 1960's War on Poverty. Columbus, Ohio was one of a 150 cities where the program was started to help the poor. Everyone knew not all poor people lived in the Model Cities area, but all people living in the Model Cities area were poor. It is amazing how labels, wherever they come from, tend to limit us if we allow them to. I know sometimes labels are placed on people so that they can receive help. But I wonder if labels are placed on people, so their mindsets are limited. In the Bible, man became a sinner due to his sin. Man being labeled as a "sinner" indicated his "condition of transgression" against God's desire that we be holy as "He is Holy." But God does not desire that man would remain in that "condition," but that man would repent and accept God's redemptive plan of salvation. Therefore, making man free to receive an unlimited mindset.

    According to sociologists, people like my wife and I were defined as "The Underclass," concentrated in the inner city, having little to no connection with the job market. Those who are employed do menial, low-paying, temporary work. For many, welfare, food stamps, and food pantries are their main support. Living in a culture of poverty breeds poor people because of their upbringing, decisions, values and norms. Sociologists focus on various components in the social structure to explain poverty (Flashcardmachine.com, Exam 2 (Essentials of Sociology)). This mumbo-jumbo says that my wife and I, the underclass (both our fathers were alcoholics), should have become underclass dysfunctional alcoholics and had very little chance for success in life. But when GOD, allows two young people to meet under such conditions, His blessings and wisdom overcomes a culture of poverty. God's vision is one of success and prosperity, not poverty and misfortune. It helps when those young people did not limit themselves according to the labels placed on them. Charles

M. Schwab once said, "when someone puts a limit on what you will do, that person has put a limit on what you can do." John Maxwell says this, "You are only an attitude away from success" and that "success isn't accumulating possessions, wealth, or power, success is obeying God."

According to the Census Bureau's report of March 1975, the Current Population Survey, the weighted average poverty cutoff for a nonfarm family of four in 1974 was $5,038. In 1974 there were approximately 24.3 million people, or 12 percent of the population, poor by this definition. During the early 1970's, my family was receiving about $2,500 a year in welfare benefits. My mother was working at that bar for about $50-$70 a week, including tips, making about $3,500 a year. According to Census Bureau, we were not poor, even though we lived in the "Model Cities", rented a double and were on welfare. If it looks like poor, sounds like poor and lives like poor, it must be poor.

Understand, I am partially grateful for my welfare assistance. My mentality is that every cloud has a silver lining. Due to my welfare status, I was able to go to college on grants from the Federal Government and the State of Ohio. The grants covered my tuition and room. All I had to do was buy books and find food. I charged my one credit card to buy my books and lived on peanut butter sandwiches and canned fruit cocktail. I worked two and three part time jobs to pay off my credit card. At the start of the next school's quarter, I would repeat the process of charging my card and paying it off. I was so glad when my girlfriend (later wife) attended the same college because she could afford room and board and had a meal plan. She worked in the cafeteria and gave me her meal ticket almost daily. Why wouldn't I marry a woman like that? After graduating from college, I owed the stupendous amount of money, a grand total of $166.19. It took me 3 years to pay off the loan. Well, my wife paid it off. She said I refused to pay the student loan. No, I was under the influence of poverty thinking, that I should not be giving to the government, the government should be giving to me.

I am not certain what all of this means, but I thought it was interesting. According to an article printed in the Weekly Standard. The Census's American Community Survey reported "the number of households with incomes below the poverty line in 2011 was 16,807,795," the Senate Budget Committee notes, "if you divide total federal and state spending by the number of households with incomes below the poverty line, the average spending per household in poverty was $61,194 in 2011." This kind of stuff bugs me, even though I grew up on welfare. Additionally, the U.S. Census Bureau reported that the real median household income in the United States in 2011 was $50,054, a 1.5 percent decline from the 2010 median and the second consecutive annual drop. How about that, the federal and state governments, on average, spent more per poor family than what the average hard-working family earned. This is so wrong in so many ways, if I started on it, I would have to write another book to fully express my opinion. But, just let me ask this, like Clair McKascal asked in the burger commercial "Where's the beef?" Well, where's the incentive? And that is on both, the poor and the average working families. If the government is going to provide, what is the use of working to get average? Why should anyone work when they can get average for free? Look, people cannot become what they need to be, as long as the Government keeps them where they are; dependent and poor. Unfortunately, there are Americans who feel as though they are entitled to free. How entitled are becoming as Americans.

I now realize, what Sir Richard Francis Burton said about poor being a state of mind is so true. Got poor? Change the state of your mind. How do you get out of the state of poor? You move to the state of prosperity. There are plenty of former poor people there. If you take Thankful Highway, you will be there before you know it. When we give thanks to God, we are acknowledging that he has given us something of value, and when we have things of value, we are not poor. Got poor? Be thankful and change the state of your mind. And when you change the state of your mind, everything else will follow.

REFLECTIONS

Do you have a rich or poor mindset?

Are you thankful for what you have?

Do you pray to God for more money to solve your situation?

Got Debt?

Train up a child in the way he should go and when he is old he will not depart from it. The rich rules over the poor and the borrower is the slave to the lender (Proverbs 22:6-7 RSV).

When I was a young lad, about 18 years old, I was trying to date my wife (girl-friend then). I thought if I bought her a sweetheart ring, she would continue to date me despite some of my strange southern ways and language. Since we lived next door to each other, she did not understand me "chucking" rocks at the cat-sized alley rats or "toting" her books from school. So, when I went to JC Penny to buy a ring, I did not have the $59 to buy the heart shaped ring with a unique diamond. I think it was called a "chip" diamond. Of course, JCP asked me if I have a credit card and I said "no," and they said, "would you like one?" At that time, I don't think anyone in my family had a credit card. I thought a credit card was something that only rich white people had. Definite not poor black people from the ghetto. We were so poor, we couldn't even afford credit. So, I asked how do I get one of these prestigious items. They said establish credit by going into debt. "And how do I do that," I asked. "By buying something on credit and paying it off," JCP said. That way, I could establish a credit (debt) history and show the credit card companies how good a credit (debt) risk I was. So, I went to a jewelry store and found the same sweetheart ring for $79 and purchased it on credit(debt). I put $20 down and made monthly payments until it was paid off. Then I went back to JCP and applied (begged) for a credit card. When I received the card in the mail, we celebrated by going to JC Penney and buying more stuff. Hallelujah!

Shucks, if I can get one, I should be able to get two. So, I went to my bank and applied (begged) for a Master Card. I did not know anything specifically about the different brands of credit cards, but I did like the word "Master." Had I only known which of us would become the master and the other the slave. I learned that you can only have a master, if you have a slave. Maybe I was not the first person in my family to have a credit card, but I don't remember anyone else having one. If they did, they did like I did and kept the cards to themselves. I might not have been the sharpest knife in the drawer, but I knew better than to let my credit cards out of my sight or to openly let someone use them. Oh, by the way, I did have a job when I obtained my credit cards.

Of course, I wanted to live out the American dream of buying a nice car and a house with a white picket-fence. Well, maybe not the house, but definitely the car. Up until 1975, I had owned four vehicles, which I had paid cash for: a 1965 Chevy (which I put in my total life savings of $69.53) purchased with other family members. When the car died and the family had abandoned it, I resurrected the car and claimed it as my own; a 1955 Chevy classic, which I paid $400 cash; a 1967 Ford Thunder Bird luxury vehicle because my momma said I should buy it. Never go car shopping with your momma, self-explanatory, plus it's not manly; and finally, a 1963 Chevy Bel-Air, which I paid $93.53, form a local car lot. I tried to always keep it moving because it smoked so bad that when I stopped, it would disappear in a cloud of smoke. So, I went to a nice car lot and picked out a car in my budgeted amount of $1,000. I had about $400 to put down on the vehicle. The salesman told me he could do the deal, "if I got a co-signer." Two problems; first, no one in my family had credit enough to co-sign for me and secondly this was something I wanted to do by myself. I wish I had been spiritually wise at the age of 20 to have known Proverbs 17:18 (KJV), *"A man void of understanding striketh hands, and becometh surety in the presence of his friend."* Some translations say you are stupid to take on someone's debt. I know the scripture says friend or neighbor, but I am throwing family in there also. Sometimes family (just in case one of them buy's this book, I am not talking about my family) can be the worst culprit in a co-signer deal. I once co-signed with family members for a television for our mother and ended up paying for most of it. I ain't mad at anyone, it's the Bible doing what it always does, come true. I refused to get a co-signer and threatened the salesman that I would go elsewhere. He laughed and said, "go ahead, you'll be back because the other places will also require a co-signer." I did go to other car lots, I cannot remember how many. As the other lots asked for more money down or a co-signer, that salesman's word began to haunt me, "you'll be back." Well I did not go back to that salesman because I found a car lot that accepted my deal without a co-signer. I became the proud owner of a 1969 Plymouth Belvedere. That slant six-engine rocked.

 Overall, I must say that I did not go crazy with my credit cards. After the first few purchases, I did understand that "Massa Card"(this is the term I like to use), did not care about my circumstances, situations, gender status, socioeconomic background, my girlfriend or that I was a member of the National Honor Society (high school). "Massa Card" just wanted me to make the payments.

 After graduating from college in 1979, I married my high school sweetheart. I remember preparing for the wedding on a "pay as we go" plan. With minimum use of our credit cards, we paid about $2,000 (including rings) for our wedding and reception. I know you are asking, "what kind of a wedding could they have had for a $2,000?" Listen, whereas my Mother was lacking as car buyer, she excelled in cooking. She cooked and froze food for months. A good friend paid for the club house where we had the reception. My wife did much of the decorating. She borrowed her sister's old wedding dress and her sister paid for our hotel room on our honeymoon. Can you say frugal? We just had to pay for gas, food and entertainment (which between any newlyweds, should be easy to figure out).

When we returned from our honeymoon, I found out I had lost my job at the local zinc manufacturing plant. Thus, began the realities of a young married couple trying to make it in life. We had a small upstairs apartment in Columbus, Ohio that we paid $35 a month. For months, I put out an endless number of resumes, but found nothing. During the absence of employment, I had nearly maxed out the Master Card. My young wife found a part time job at a downtown department store. One evening she got off work and came home to one of my specialty dinners I had prepared. There were candle lights, salad and spaghetti and wieners (what did you expect, filet Mignon?). The dinner was romantic and was going very well until my wife wanted to watch television and I had to tell her we had no electrical power. The candle light dinner was the result of the electrical company shutting off our electricity because I had not paid the bill. I was embarrassed and humbled. A month later my wife was pregnant, part of that entertainment I guess. Big time college graduate, broke, busted, disgusted and sitting in the dark, but God. The Bible says we are never forsaken nor forgotten. Before that month was over, I had received job offers from a local department store (detective), another job offered was a county deputy (jailer) and another as a state undercover investigator. God is Good. In November 1979, I started my job with the state of Ohio Department of Liquor Control.

As so many young couples, we struggled financially, but we made it. The world does not stop because you struggle, have a baby, lose a job or lose a parent. The world keeps on going and that is what young couples have to do, keep on going. We lost one of our parents and several grandparents in the early years of our marriage. I remember driving non-stop (22 hours) from Ohio to Texas on a few occasions. We did not stop because hotel stays were not in my mentality nor was it in our budget. Then on one trip, my wife said, we are not driving non-stop, well let me quote her, "I am not driving without stopping so, we are going to get a hotel." I argued (since I was the driver) that I did not need a hotel room. She said fine, I could sleep in the car, but she and our new baby son were sleeping in the hotel. It is amazing that at first, we did not have the money to do so, however when my wife said to stop, we had the money for a hotel. Gentlemen let me tell you something, a good wife has a stash of cash somewhere. *"The heart of her husband trusts in her, and he will have no lack of gain,"* (Proverbs 31:11, RSV). She saves the stash for family emergencies. On another similar trip, there were about seven of us traveling in a single vehicle. We pulled into a hotel for the night and my cousin from Texas asked what we were doing. My mother, who was aware of our use of hotels told her that is what we (me and my wife) did, we slept in hotels. My cousin accused us of thinking that we were rich. That was the first time anyone had called us rich, but since it was from a poor thinking cousin, it really did not count.

I left the state of Ohio for a position with the U.S. Border Patrol. My wife, our first born and I moved to Del Rio, Texas in 1982. I remember it was just before Christmas and we were driving to Del Rio. We were out in the middle of Nowhere, Texas. Now you might ask is there such a place called Nowhere, Texas? Let me tell you, there are a lot of places called Nowhere, Texas. Whether you say, we are now here in Texas or you say, we are in no-where Texas, it's all the same. My wife looked over at me and asked me if I knew where I was going. She later told me, she thought we were driving off the end of the world. We arrived in Del Rio with no debt (my wife made sure of that), a small Uhaul trailer and about $2,000 from a state of Ohio retirement fund. Six months later, we had an apartment furnished and our little savings had diminished to zero dollars. Every chance we had to get socialization, we would go to a "real" city like San Antonio and get big city socialization. When our friends would ask why we went to San Antonio so often, I would tell them that it was the nearest place where we could buy "Afro-Sheen" hair dressing for my hair (that's a hair joke because I am bald as an eight ball). After living in Del Rio for two years, we did not amass any wealth, nor did we go to the poor farm. We did like many other young couples, we survived.

Halfway between San Antonio and Del Rio was a town named Uvalde, Texas. Historically, Uvalde is known as the Honey Capital because of its world production of huajillo, a mild, light-colored honey, dating back to the 1870s. Like it talks about in the Bible a land flowing with milk and honey. There was a sign just as you entered Uvalde that said, "Welcome to God's Country." To me, Uvalde looked like a nice place to live, green, pleasant and full of life. However, God's Blessing seem to stop in Uvalde and did not reach the Banks family in Del Rio. It seems we had everything but, life and life more abundantly. Del Rio just wasn't my wife's cup of tea. It was not her land of milk and honey but was her wilderness. She became pregnant and refused to have our second child in the state of Texas. So, we went back to Ohio to have our baby. Of course, everything worked out well and we had much our family there in Columbus. I had to go back and forth between Columbus and Del Rio several times. Since we did not have an emergency fund, in that light, neither did we have a savings, traveling, sinking, house or any other fund, in fact, we didn't even have a budget. Therefore, we used our good old "Massa Card." We did not get into a lot of debt, but it was more than we should have gotten into. Listen young people, the greatest thing you can have as a young couple or is not the hottest sex life, not the most stuff, it's not enough money or even the coolest ministry, it's not even attending a great church. It's wisdom. Wisdom will take you further in life than any of those things. Proverbs (3:16 CEV) says, *"In her right-hand Wisdom hold a long life, and in her left hand are wealth and honor."*

Ultimately, I got a job with a Department of Defense agency as a Special Agent. The first assignment was at the Naval Air Station (NAS) Corpus Christi, TX. Our next assignment was a tour in the Naval Station, Philippines, where we were able to save about $17,000. We thought we were rolling in dough. We had it until we got to our following assignment, Naval Training Center, Great Lakes (Chicago), IL. We quickly put down most of that money on a $120K house. My wife worked part time jobs here and there during the marriage, but had agreed to be a stay at home mother and home school our children (God bless her). This was an absolute blessing to our family and hard work for her. Therefore, we had to operate on one income. For the most part, we maintained a $2-3K balance on the one "Massa Card." We would pay it off and then charge it up again. In 1994, God laid upon my heart to get our finances right and to author a financial study to share with the church we were attending. I created something I called "Financial Stewardship (Riches take wings and fly away)." In Financial Stewardship, I said stewardship was simply, "properly using what God has given us." In it, I also cited that the Biblical uses of money were to; Honor God, provide for self and family, and to Help others. One Wednesday night, the Pastor of the church where my family attended, allowed me conduct the financial teaching to the members. I was talking about financial strategies (methods) members of the congregations had employed to save money. No one said anything. You would have thought I asked them to give me the recipe for the atomic bomb. The pastor of the church nervously scratched his eyebrow at the lack of responses. The best example that I came up with, at that moment (of distress), was that we reused paper hand towels to wipe up spills on the floor. Then someone turned to my wife and said, "aren't you glad he doesn't make you reuse toilet paper." The Lord probably smiled at my little effort and said, the boy is trying.

We transferred to Kansas City, Kansas, on September 11, 2000. There we did very well with our finances. We had saved enough money from the sale of our house in Chicago to pay cash for a new mini-van. We paid off credit cards and all debts, paying our tithes and offerings and being blessed by God. In 2003, we got a pay raise of about $150 a month and we refinanced our house and saved another $150 a month. You know what this meant? Car time! So, we bought a new 2003 Saturn Vue. I think in life, a good vision leads to a good view, so we all should have a good view (Vue) in life. Sorry, I couldn't resist the play on words. We Christians all like to say that God blessed us with our new car, then we go and make our monthly payments for 72 months. After 6 months of making payments, we began complaining about our claimed blessing and having sorrows about the purchase. But Proverbs says that the blessing of God have no sorrows.

In the fall of 2003 I transferred to Austin, TX. Even though it was for my job, the Government did not pay for the move, so we had to. Nor did the Government pay for the sale of our house. Unfortunately, I jumped the gun and bought a house in Texas after receiving a bid on our house in Kansas City. The problem was I did a "surprise" buy for our anniversary, of the house in Texas. I put a contract on the Texas house on a Friday. The man who placed a bid on our house in Kansas City called that Saturday to tell me that he could not buy our house because he had lost his job. That was not just a "bummer," it was a kick in the anatomy that makes you double over and want to throw-up. Now all was not lost. When I had placed the bid on the house in Texas, I had made it so low, the realtor indicated that only with God's intervention would the accepted bid be approved. So, while enjoying our anniversary weekend, the realtor called and said "it must have been a Divine intervention because the bid was accepted, and you got the house." I must have had this "wow" look on my face when my wife asked me who had called, and I told her it was the realtor from Texas. Then my lovely, precious, almost all knowing, Holy Ghost filled wife said, "aren't you glad we didn't buy that house in Texas?" I felt so small, I could have walked through the eye of a needle. Embarrassed, I said "surprise!" Things went dark shortly thereafter, I did not see if it was a right hook or a straight left that got me. Well, enough about that. Life is like box of chocolates. Now we were committed to move, against my wife's intuition or feeling. A wise and rich man said, "never go against your wife's feelings or it's going to cost you in the end." Well, we moved to Austin, Texas. Because we had so much stuff (a condition called stuffitis) it was as if we moved twice. We did two separate moves; we leased two trucks, two car carriers, rented hotels for the two moves and now had two houses. Even as I am typing this, and my wife is looking at me, I feel as if I need to duck.

 We rolled into Austin Texas with only a car debt of about $15,000, not bad. Then we added to the debt, about $10,000 for our move (that's what I told the IRS and I am sticking with it). Added to our monthly budget were two utilities, two HOA payments (don't get me started with the HOA), several trips back to KC to check on the house, two house payments, a back yard that needed a yard for that Austin house (I should have told that realtor, no back yard, no front pay), and most of all window treatments. I don't call blinds and curtains "treatments," they are more like surgery, because they cut deep into our non-existing reservoir of money.

Now to come up with the $50,000 down payment for our $300,000 Texas home (things might be bigger in Texas, but they ain't always cheaper), we did a home equity loan on the house in Kansas. Therefore, when we sold our house in Kansas in April 2004, we cleared enough money to pay for the hotel and gas back to Texas. The home equity loan was another example of not having a long-term plan to buy a house. Listen to the voice of regret and don't do it the way I did it. Notice how I kept my wife out of the mess.

Within our first several months in Texas, we were $27,000 in debt. Our two youngest were being home schooled. That was another couple of thousand dollars for their curriculums. Our property taxes for our first year was about $5000. Man, I knew it would be higher than the $2800 taxes in Kansas, so I was content, until I received a tax bill from the local independent school district of $5000. Really? Really? Really? I became an instant tax revolter. Being a believer in my Lord and Savior Jesus Christ was the only saving grace that I did not lead a one-man tax riot. I have not used a string of sentences consisting foul, cursive, explicative language ever in my life, as I thought of using the day I received that tax bill. It still spins me up today when I think about it. It is a good thing that Jesus said *"Pay to Caesar the things that belong to Caesar. Pay to God the things that belong to God,* (Matthew 22:21)." Thank you Lord, but that still doesn't stop me from spinning, y'all pray for me please. Anyway, at the end of our first Texas year, we were easily about $30,000 in the red and we had not vacationed in Cancun, lived the high life or even bought a flat screen television. Now don't get me wrong, our house was pretty nice, 3611 square feet, 5 bed - 4 bath, 3 car garage, etc. Of course, the county taxed us on 3900 square feet, more spinning for me. Our neighborhood was a top community in our area and had a representation of being a "snooty" community. One day, I look around at my neighbors and noticed something about the cars our neighbors' kids were driving. I'm talking about high school kids, I'm talking about kids, man, high school kids. The cars they were driving were better than mine. I had to do something. Here we go. Can you say, "increase my income?" The Government wasn't offering any more money. That meant, home based business. I started selling health juice. Healthy for their bank account, not for mine. Somehow, we slipped further into the red. How about flipping homes? My wife asked me if I knew what I was doing. Was she kidding or what? I had been to that free real estate seminar and had even paid $1,000.00 for those weekend classes (further in the red). I was ready or as ready as I was ever going to be. I was going to be a quick house flipper. We bought a house (that my wife was not in favor of). I worked like a knucklehead renovating that house after working my regular job. I tried to sell that house quickly, did not work. I tried to rent it, did not work. I got a realtor and 10 months later, sold that house. On paper, I made $2,000.00 when all was said and done. My quick flip had turned into a slow roll. In actuality, the double rent, utilities, taxes, etc. meant more red ink. I was trying to make more money for our household. My wife finally said "stop trying to make us more money," because it was making us more broke.

From 2003 to 2006, if you were to add up our total debt, to include three houses, one car, triple utilities, triple taxes, rehab costs, trying to help our children with college costs, everyday living stuff and topping it off, being house poor, we had over $473,000 in debt (not all at one time). When you take out the mortgage debt, we were over $80,000 in the red. Like most of America (70%), we were living from pay check to pay check. Skimping and scraping just to get by. But, we were living in one of the nicest subdivisions in Austin, Texas in a nice big house. When I mentioned that it must have been Divine intervention that we were able to buy that house, the book of Proverbs (10:22 (NKJV) says *"The blessing of the Lord makes one rich, and He adds no sorrow with it."* I thought that the house was a blessing, I mean we got it for $38,000 less than what they were asking for it. I figured that if it looked like a blessing, sounded like a blessing and saved me a dollar, it must have been a blessing. Plus, between the realtor and the title people, they said for the first year, our payments would be quite affordable. We were making about $92,000 a year and were bringing home about $6,000 a month. According to financial experts, your monthly mortgage/rent should be no more than 25-30 percent of your take home pay. This equated to what should have been a mortgage payment of about $1,500-$1,800 a month. Well, our first year, we were about $2,000 a month. Now I ain't the brightest bulb plugged in, but I knew $2,000 a month was too low an amount to be paying for that $250,000 mortgage we had on our house. I repeatedly contacted the title company and asked them to recalculate the mortgage. We even asked the bank, nothing changed. I learned that these institutions sometime (often) keep payments low the first year to get buyers into the house. Once you have filled-up your garage with all of your stuff, you really don't want to move that stuff for a while. Then comes the surprise. See, after being in the house for six to twelve months, the financial institutions then recalculate your mortgage escrow and guess what, it normally goes up. After the first year and the recalculation, the bank sent us our new mortgage payment coupon booklet for $3,100 a month. Two things kept me from going through the roof: First I couldn't afford to repair the roof of a new house, and secondly, we had somewhat anticipated the shortage to our escrow and had put several thousand dollars aside. Then we filed homestead to help reduce the mortgage, we talked to the bank and arranged to pay the set aside money into our escrow. By doing this, we reduced our monthly escrow payment to about $2,500. This caused our budget to be assuredly out of balance. Over the next several years, we entwined ourselves into a condition of being "house poor." And when you are house poor, you always have wants and needs. Well we were so broke, we could not afford the wants, so we had to address the needs. You see, needs won't keep, something must be done about them or the needs become emergencies. And we Americans know how to handle emergencies when we have no money, we charge (with credit) and go deeper in debt.

In 2006, my wife had had just about enough of living pay check to pay check. Every time we would scrape together a little savings some situation would come along and it would be gone. Seemingly, every paycheck had someone else's name on it before it hit our kitchen table. We paid our tithes and offerings, but where were the men giving into our bosom, shaken down pressed together and over flowing? I really was trying to remedy the situation, but bottom line was the lack of cash-ola, mula, lettuce, scratch, bucks, dinero, and anything else that would spend, kept us going in circles. Now our debt was tearing at the relationship between my wife and I, which then affected the entire family. We had to stop doing the same thing, hoping for something different. We needed to change the things, our habits, in order to change our finances. Bruce Barton said, "When you're through changing, you're through." We were just beginning to be through.

"We first form habits, then habits form us," (John Maxwell).

TBanks

REFLECTIONS

What habits did you form that helped you get into debt? List your debts and their balances. Did you need or want all of these? This will help you to know your finances.

Debt Types	Balances	Need or Want

Know Your Flocks and Your Herds

Proverbs 27:23-24 (NKJV)
23 *Be diligent to know the state of your flocks, And attend to your herds;*
24 *For riches are not forever, Nor does a crown endure to all generations.*

As a child, we lived in a poor rural area in Texas. How poor were we? We were so poor that when we played kick the can down the dirt road, people thought we were moving. We were so poor that when you walked through our front door and closed it, you were standing on our back porch. We had no windowpanes in our windows, mosquitoes would drain us of our blood. We would then herd them into one windowless room, catch them, drain them of their blood and sell the blood to Red Cross. We were so poor, that our pigs brought us food, so poor that Colonel Sanders donated his chicken heads and feet, just so we would have something to eat; and a million more so poor jokes. Those were jokes, but the truth of the matter; we did use cow patties (dung) as frisbees. About a third of the panes in our house were missing from our windows, and to survive we had to sleep under the covers or the mosquitoes would drain us dry of blood. Our house had no running water nor bathroom and we could not even afford an outhouse, we had to use other folk's bathrooms (outhouses). We really had a pig that lived under our house. I did eat food out of the garbage buckets which was meant for the hogs. And them ain't no poor jokes. Anyway, I was exposed, in more ways than one, to farm living. When I heard some say that one of the biggest problems we have with our finances is that we have fail to focus or pay attention to our money, the above proverb hit home. Bu-yah! Let me explain.

Let's look at Dictionary.com to give us a knowledgeable perspective of the above verse. Diligent - constant in effort to accomplish something; attentive and persistent in doing anything: a diligent student. Done or pursued with persevering attention; painstaking: a diligent search of the files.

Know the state - condition; a particular mode of being of a person or thing; existing state; situation with respect to circumstances. A circumstance indispensable to some result; prerequisite; that on which something else is contingent:

Attend - to be present at: to go with as a concomitant or result; accompany: to take care of; minister to; devote ones services to: to wait upon; accompany as a companion or servant: to take charge of; watch over; look after; tend; guard.

Flock - a number of animals of one kind, especially sheep, goats, or birds, that keep or feed together or are herded together. a large number of people; crowd. a large group of things: to gather or go in a flock or crowd:

Herd - a number of animals kept, feeding, or traveling together; drove; flock: a herd of cattle; a herd of sheep; a herd of zebras. Sometimes Disparaging. a large group of people:

any large quantity: rabble: He had no opinions of his own, but simply followed the herd.

"Be diligent to know the state of your flocks, and attend to your herds;" When I look at this scripture, and the first word is "be." I have learned that in order to be successful, I must stop being what I am and become the "be" that God is instructing me to become. Therefore, I must be constant in an effort to accomplish something. The something for me is being aware of the certain conditions and/or existing circumstances of my flocks. And, then to watch over, look after, take charge of and if necessary accompany or devote my services to my herds. What the flock and what the herd?

Flocks and Herds

I know the Bible is talking about my money, well our money, OK, OK, well God's money. Haggai 2:8 (NKJV) says, *"The silver is Mine, the gold is Mine, says the Lord of Host."* If you had any doubts, let them be gone. It's all God's money. It be not yo money, yo mommas money, yo old man's money, not even your worked fo money, it's God's money. "Be diligent to know the state of your flocks, and attend to your herds; For riches are not forever, Nor does a crown endure to all generations." Now I might not be the sharpest knife in the drawer, but I did figure out this verse. I know it's talking about money because first of all, the next verse starts out saying "For riches." Secondly, in agrarian cultures, a person's wealth was based on his possessions, most often his flocks and herds of livestock. In Genesis, chapter 13:2 (KJV), the Bible says that "Abram was very rich in livestock, in silver, and in gold." We know this livestock (wealth) consisted of sheep, oxen, male donkeys, female donkeys, camels, and male and female servants (Gen. 12:16, 20:14, 24:35). In Job, the first chapter, the Bible says that Job had among his possession seven thousand sheep, three thousand camels, oxen, female donkeys, a very large (and in charge) household, so that he was the greatest of all the people of the East. He was rolling in riches. Then God and the accuser of the brethren made a little wager. The next thing you know Job lost all he had due to an accusation from the accuser. That's why it is not wise to go to Vegas, because often, what is bet in Vegas, stays in Vegas. My Father-n-law used to say, "if you want to double your money, fold it in half and put it back into your pocket." In the last chapter of Job, his possessions were restored, doubled. He had fourteen thousand sheep. Who counted all of those sheep? Don't forget Solomon. In addition to great wisdom, God gave him riches and honor. He had forty thousand stalls for his horses. Who counted all of those horses? Anyway, point made. Little flocks and herds, little dinero. Mas grande flocks and herds, mucho dinero.

God is saying "be" diligent to know, "be" attentive to your riches, whatever that might be. My theory (Theodorology) says these riches could include my livestock, wealth, family, business, workers, etc. You see, my good friend Webster defines riches as abundant possessions, wealth; abundance of whatever is precious. But, "be" diligent means focused, attend to it or take charge over it. If we become the opposite of "be," being or existing, we are not diligent and do not watch over or take care of our possessions.

When I was about 8 years old, two of my brothers (Greg and Joe) and I, would spend the weekends at our Father's house in the country. It was the same house we lived in when he was married to our mom. Our dad had not completed any improvements on the house in some years. It still had no running water or no bathroom on about three acres of land. Now our father was seldom there on the weekends with us, to which we rejoiced. No supervision. We would get up in the morning about 10:00am, eat cereal, play with our cousins all day long, and eat hot dogs at night. What a life. Our dad had several calves and our only instructions were to feed the calves in the morning and in the evening. Our mornings were a lot later than sunrise mornings and our evenings were more like nighttime feeding. The calves decided to look for more consistent meals elsewhere. They broke through the fence and tried to eat our neighbor's house. The neighbors called our dad, he came and gave us a stern talking to. We were not diligent or attentive, let alone knowing where those calves had gone. And like those calves, if left alone, our riches will get away from us. Proverbs 23:4-5 (NKJV) says: *"Do not overwork to be rich; Because of your own understanding, cease! Will you set your eyes on that which is not? For riches certainly make themselves wings; They fly away like an eagle toward heaven."* God did not say go crazy-diligent, or be only diligent on your money (then you get out of balance by focusing more on your money than on God) and that's a no-no. Why? Because it's not your money.

Proverbs 27:24a (NKJV), *"For riches are not forever."* Sarah Schmalbruch for the Business Insider Jul. 13, 2015, In an article titled "9 rich and famous people who filed for bankruptcy" told how people like rapper 50 Cent was once worth $155 million; when rapper MC Hammer released his hit album "Please Hammer Don't Hurt 'Em" in 1990, Forbes estimated his income at $33 million that year, but in 1996, Hammer filed for bankruptcy protection with a total of $1 million in assets and at least $10 million in debts; When Francis Ford Coppola filed for bankruptcy protection in 1992, for the second time, his assets were listed at $52 million and liabilities at $98 million, according to the New York Times; former MLB pitcher Curt Schilling earned just over $114 million during his 19-year career, ESPN reported, but after a $50 million investment went bust, he filed bankruptcy in 2012. He was forced to sell many of his possessions (including his famous bloody sock and his $3 million Massachusetts home); Mike Tyson earned a staggering $400 million over the course of his 20-year boxing career, according to the New York Times, he filed for bankruptcy in 2003, with a total of $23 million in debt. His debts included a $9 million divorce settlement, $13.4 million to the IRS, and $4 million to the British tax authorities; and many more. According to the Merna Law Firm, there were over 930,000 bankruptcy filings in 2014. Remember, riches are not forever and even shorter if we are not being diligent with and attending to our flocks and herds. Your flocks and herds will make a difference in your life if you personally attend to them.

Proverb 27:24b (NKJV), *"Nor does a crown endure to all generations."* Natalie Robehmed, Forbes, wrote an article, "The Vanderbilts: How American Royalty Lost Their Crown Jewels." In the article, she wrote how Cornelius 'Commodore' Vanderbilt began the family business by borrowing $100 from his mother and piloting a passenger boat on Staten Island in 1810. And expanded into steamboats and built a railroads empire. By the time of his death in 1877, he reportedly had accumulated a $100 million fortune, more than was held in the U.S. Treasury at the time. The article went on to say the second generation doubled the family's fortune but it was the third generation who stopped growing the fortune; there was gambling and neglect in the fourth generation and the fifth generation filed bankruptcy. Crowns do not always endure to the next generation, especially if we are not being diligent and attentive.

Sheep and goats

Proverbs 27:25(NKJV): *"When the hay is removed, and the tender grass shows itself,*

And the herbs of the mountains are gathered in, 26: The lambs will provide your clothing,

And the goats the price of a field; 27: You shall have enough goats milk for your food,

For the food of your household, And the nourishment of your maidservants."

When we look at these next few scriptures, we understand that flocks and herds refer to lambs (sheep) and goats. According to Wikipedia (the free encyclopedia), things to know about sheep and goats. Sheep are quadrupedal, ruminant mammals typically kept as livestock. An adult female sheep is referred to as a ewe, an intact male as a ram or occasionally a tup, a castrated male as a wether, and a younger sheep as a lamb. Colors of domestic sheep range from pure white to dark chocolate brown and even spotted or piebald (having patches of other colors). White wool is desirable for large commercial markets, there is a niche market for colored fleeces, mostly for hand spinning. Sheep are an important part of the global agricultural economy. Sheep also play a major role in many local economies, which may be niche markets focused on organic or sustainable agriculture and local food customers. Especially in developing countries, such flocks may be a part of subsistence agriculture rather than a system of trade. Sheep themselves may be a medium of trade in barter economies. Domestic sheep provide a wide array of raw materials. Wool was one of the first textiles, although in the late 20th century wool prices began to fall dramatically as the result of the popularity and cheap prices for synthetic fabrics. For many sheep owners, the cost of shearing is greater than the possible profit from the fleece, making subsistence on wool production alone practically impossible without farm subsidies. Fleeces are used as material in making alternative products such as wool insulation.

In the 21st century, the sale of meat is the most profitable enterprise in the sheep industry, even though far less sheep meat is consumed than chicken, pork or beef. Sheepskin is likewise used for making clothes, footwear, rugs, and other products. By-products from the slaughter of sheep are also of value: sheep tallow can be used in candle and soap making, sheep bone and cartilage has been used to furnish carved items such as dice and buttons as well as rendered glue and gelatin. Sheep intestine can be formed into sausage casings, and lamb intestine has been formed into surgical sutures, as well as strings for musical instruments and tennis rackets. Even sheep droppings, which are high in cellulose, have been sterilized and mixed with traditional pulp materials to make paper. Of all sheep by-products, perhaps the most valuable is lanolin: the waterproof, fatty substance found naturally in sheep's wool and used as a base for innumerable cosmetics and other products.

A new option for deriving profit from live sheep is the rental of flocks for grazing; these "mowing services" are hired in order to keep unwanted vegetation down in public spaces and to lessen fire hazard. They do not require the expensive housing, such as that used in the intensive farming of chickens or pigs. They are an efficient use of land. Roughly six sheep can be kept on the amount that would suffice for a single cow or horse. Sheep can also consume plants, such as noxious weeds, that most other animals will not touch, and produce more-young at a faster rate. In contrast to most livestock species, the cost of raising sheep is not necessarily tied to the price of feed crops such as grain, soybeans and corn. Combined with the lower cost of quality sheep, all these factors combine to equal a lower overhead for sheep producers, thus entailing a higher profitability potential for the small farmer.

According to Wikipedia, the domestic goat is a subspecies of goat domesticated from the wild goat of southwest Asia and Eastern Europe. The goat is closely related to the sheep as both are in the goat-antelope subfamily Capri-nae. There are over 300 distinct breeds of goat. Goats are one of the oldest domesticated species, and have been used for their milk, meat, hair, and skins over much of the world. In 2011, there were more than 922 million live goats around the globe, according to the UN Food and Agriculture Organization. Female goats are referred to as does or nannies, intact males as bucks, billies, or rams and their offspring are kids. Castrated males are wethers. Goat meat from younger animals are called kid or cabrito (Spanish), and from older animals is simply known as goat or sometimes called chevon (French), or in some areas mutton (which more often refers to adult sheep meat). A goat is useful to humans when it is living and when it is dead, first as a renewable provider of milk, manure, and fiber, and then as meat and hide. Some charities provide goats to impoverished people in poor countries, because goats are easier and cheaper to manage than cattle and have multiple uses. In addition, goats are used for driving and packing purposes. The intestine of goats is used to make "catgut", which is still in use as a material for internal human surgical sutures and strings for musical instruments. The horn of the goat, which signifies plenty and well-being (the cornucopia), is also used to make spoons.

Goats are mentioned many times in the Bible. A goat is considered a "clean" animal by Jewish dietary laws and was slaughtered for an honored guest. It was also acceptable for some kinds of sacrifices. Goat-hair curtains were used in the tent that contained the tabernacle (Exodus 25:4(CEV)). Its horns can be used instead of sheep's horn to make a shofar. On Yom Kippur, the festival of the Day of Atonement, two goats were chosen and lots were drawn for them. One was sacrificed and the other allowed to escape into the wilderness, symbolically carrying with it the sins of the community. From this comes the word "scapegoat."

Why all these words on Mary's little lamb? Wait, scratch that. Mary's Little Lamb is the Word and there is a lot to say about Him. Let me rephrase that. Why all the verbosity about Lambsy Pie and cousin Billy goat? When you only see a cute little woolly animal or a little animal with horns and a goatee, then it is likely that when you see a dollar bill, then you probably only see a dollar bill. If that is the case, then you are missing what the Word of God is saying. Because the lamb was not just a lamb, according to the Bible (when we be diligent to know and are attentive), it is a source of provision. When I look at a lamb, I don't see dice, nor do I think of the casinos. I don't see candles and bars of soap, nor carved items like buttons or sheep glue (making gorillas mad) or gelatin. I didn't know that sheep intestine was formed into sausage casings and lamb intestine formed into sutures, strings for musical instruments and tennis rackets. And that sheep droppings are used to make to make paper (makes me look at a sheet of paper differently). Now, I did think of the sheep mowing services, but thought the Home Owners Associations (HOA) would have problems with it. Plus, I did not want to deal with all that - paper making stuff on my lawn.

The book of Proverbs showed me that a goat was not just a goat (when we be diligent to know and are attentive), it paid for the purchase of land, and provided milk, food and nourishment for one's family and servants. When I look at a goat, I don't see charitable solutions to impoverished people in poor countries. I didn't know the intestine of a goat is used to make surgical sutures and strings for musical instruments or that the horn of the goat is also used to make spoons. (Now I have to watch what I eat with.) The horn of the goat signifies plenty and well-being.

So, now when we see sheep and goats, we should see finances and dollars. And when we see a dollar, we should see our four supportive walls; food, shelter, utilities and transportation. We should see education, employment, tools, better communities, cities, nations, happiness, vacations, meeting the needs of others. We should see children and grandchildren, romantic evenings, and church growth. With a dollar we can build things like hospitals, community centers, churches and homes. With a dollar we can pay for things like food and clothes for the homeless, for a missionary's need overseas, or your tithes and offering, and much more. However, we can see these things when we "be diligent to know and are attentive" to our finances.

The book of Proverbs can be so impactful on our lives if we would read a chapter a day. Not only would one become wiser, one would obtain a master's degree in finances. Proverbs 23:5 (NIV) says *"Cast but a glance at riches and they are gone, for they certainly make themselves wings; They fly away like an eagle toward heaven."* This is scriptural and all so sensible. See that eagle on your dollar bill, it has wings. If you only glance at it and don't give it some acknowledgement - be diligent to know, the wings come out and it's gone. I don't know about you, but I have asked my wife and she has asked me, "what happened to the money?" As if some magician came into our house, waved his wand and puff, the money disappeared. Well, now we know, it took wings and flew away. We fixed that, we closed our windows. How did we close the windows? We started being diligent with God's money, our finances, being attentive to it and handling it. Telling the money where to go. Now sometime, our riches go to heaven, to mortgage, to utilities, to Aunt Juju or to pay off debt. Now that we understand our need to be diligent, we get to tell the money where to go.

After about the fifth time reading Proverbs 27:23(NKJV), I began to understand scripturally what Dave Ramsey and others meant when they said the biggest problem with people and their finances is that people have not paid attention to their finances. Proverbs 20:4(NIV), says: *"Sluggards do not plow in season so at harvest time they look but find nothing.* The Message (MSG) says it this way: *"A farmer too lazy to plant in the spring has nothing to harvest in the fall."* I am not calling anyone a sluggard or lazy. I know we are anything but that. We are too busy to be lazy. I cannot speak for this farmer, maybe he or she were busy digging wells, repairing the farm, or working for Uber. I do not know. A sluggard is defined as someone who is lazy or idle. Whatever the circumstances, the farmer was not being diligent in their efforts toward his field. Since this is a book on finances, you know there must be some type of correlation. "The richest soil, uncultivated, produces the rankest weeds (Plutarch)." Our finances if left uncultivated (unbudgeted) or if we never plant (invest) or at least do something (take charge of it's movement), then like the farmer, we will look for a harvest and have nothing. We must stop being sluggish with our finances. William H. Danforth said "The best cure for a sluggish mind is to disturb it's routine."

If you are not diligent with your finances, the banks (not us) will be diligent and attentive too and will taketh thy funds. If you don't have a plan, the banks got a plan. In an article titled: "FDIC study: outrageous overdraft fees" by Laura Bruce of Bankrate.com she writes "The findings of an FDIC study of bank automatic overdraft programs -- also called courtesy overdraft or bounce protection have shown them to be short-term loans that cost consumers billions in fees, while often denying them the ability to make an informed choice. In another article written in the Bloomberg Institute titled, "There's a Spot in Hell Reserved for Bank Overdraft Fees" by Ben Steverman 2014-02-27 - One study of 7,500 bank customers found that 72 percent of checking accounts drop below $100 in any given month. More than 36 million checking accounts get overdrawn each year, and 8 million account holders do so more than six times a year, according to the Center for Responsible Lending. The article reported: Most customers are unaware of the overdraft until after the transaction; this is a huge amount of money (non-interest) for the banks; and overdraft fees ranged from $10 to

$38, with a median fee of $27. These fees have been huge for banks. In 2007 consumers were paying fees of $17.5 billion annually -- on automatic overdraft loans of $15.8 billion per year. Were banks taking monies from their most desperate customers with the highest priced credit which consumers haven't applied for and didn't know they are using?" James Sterngold wrote an article in the Wall Street Journal "Banks Fee Bonanza Dries Up" in which he stated, "changes in banking rules and customer behaviors squeezed what was a key source of revenue for the banking industries." In 2009, the banking industry took in more than $41 billion in account fees. Bank fees made up from a half to three quarters of the banks' profits. Banks were reportedly collecting fees not only when there was a debit card overdraft, but would then charge the customer a transfer fee when the bank moved money over to cover the over draft. There were fees taken from accounts when the daily balance dropped below certain amounts, i.e., $100.00. With the average ATM fee at $4.35, it is easy to see how "Banks are Hazardous to Your Wealth." In 2010, the Federal Government implemented limits on fees which banks could collect from its customers. By 2013, the figures had dropped to $32.5 billion, according to the Federal Deposit Insurance Corp. Additionally, Strengold attributed customers technological advances in bringing down part of the banking revenues. With the ability to conduct banking inquiries at the touch of a bank's app, a larger percent of bank customers are moving funds to prevent overdrafts. That is a way of being diligent concerning ones finances.

Several years ago, I was looking to open a debit card account that wasn't connected to our house accounts. So, I proudly brought a Temporary Walmart Money Card (VISA). I paid $20 and there was a $3 activation fee. My need for the card never materialized so after six months I decided to reload the card to purchase something else. However, when I gave the Wal Mart clerk the VISA card, I was told the transaction could not be done and was asked to contact the retail bank. Upon contacting the bank, the bank's representative said the card could not be reloaded because the card was over drafted, and I owed the bank $4. I was confused. How could I owe when I never used the card? Then I got mad and asked the guy, "what happened to the money?" The man explained to me that there was a monthly service fee of $3 (seven months), plus a three dollars activation fee, totaling $24. He asked, "Didn't you read that on the paper work?" Well, no. I was too busy to read all that fine print stuff. Got no time to be diligent to know or pay attention to my flocks or herds. So, the guy said we will waive the $4 if I reloaded the card with more money. Fool me once, shame on you, fool me twice, shame on me. The lack of being diligent, can cost you money.

Pay attention to what you have! My wife came to me in 2006 and said "You better do something about these finances or I am going to leave you here to deal with them by yourself." She had been trying to correct our fiduciary fall, but it seems (to her) that I was moving backward and not forward toward the problem. I began to look at our finances, family and faith and I found failure. I knew we were living paycheck to paycheck and my wife was calling me to pay attention to our finances. I did, and we were in trouble. Our flocks and herds were being eaten up by predators (creditors) as fast as we were making them. Isn't it funny how similar those two terms sound, predator and creditor. The big bad wolves of our finances. We could list a number of big bad wolves that eat up our flocks and herds, that consumes our hard-earned finances. 1 John 2:16 (KJV), *"For all that is in the world, the lust of the flesh, and the lust of the eyes, and the pride of life, is not of the Father, but is of the world."*

REFLECTIONS

List your accounts and the balances in them. This will help you to know your finances.

Account Types	Balances

Now You Know – Ruminato

1Timothy 4:15 (NKJV) Meditate on these things; give yourself entirely to them, that your progress may be evident to all.

In 2006, my wife came to me with a look on her face and a stirring in her voice that I could not ignore. She said I had better do something about our finances or she would leave me, and I would have to deal with our debt by myself. We were planning a trip to the West coast. It was for my job and I had decided to drive. My wife wanted to ride-shotgun on the trip with me. Now, she really did not have a shotgun, but being from Texas, the land of gun owners (to which I am one), that's the terminology that we use. My wife made a brilliant suggestion. She said she would read a book out loud while I drove and that doing the twenty-five hours (one way) drive, we would have it read by the time we returned to Texas. She told me the name of the book was the "Total Money Makeover" by Dave Ramsey. This was the era when many makeover type reality shows were gaining popularity. I said (to myself of course) what kind of a makeover nut job was this. I had heard about Dave Ramsey and the only thing

I could recall was that he insulted people concerning their finances.

We started our trip and my wife was like a kid at Christmas, she could not wait to read the book. However, I on the other hand not so thrilled. I started out the trip talking about everything under the sun, then about everything over the sun, then about the great Texas landscape. I then noticed that all the West Texas landscape began to look the same. Brown grass, no trees, cactus and this was an hour into the trip. I saw my wife pull out the book. I began to ramble incoherently. Sweat began to roll off my forehead and then my bald head hanged low, defeated, all my procrastination had failed. She knew she had me. She read, and I drove. I drove, and she read. I drove some more, and she read even more. I am so glad that my wife does not like to drive with the dome light on at night or she might still be reading. I got some reprieve. By the end of the trip, Dave and I were friends, well to the point that he was no longer someone I had an aversion too. His book had some funny stuff in it. That kept me awake on the trip, along with my pork rinds and carmel popcorn. And of course, we discussed those Dave Ramsey's Seven Baby Steps: 1) Establish a $1,000 Emergency Fund, 2) the Debt Snowball, 3) 3 to 6 Months of Expenses Emergency Fund, 4)15% Investment for Retirement, 5) College Saving for Children,6) Pay Off Home and 7) Build Wealth and Give it Away.

The first thing to turning around any situation is not coming up with a plan. The first thing is knowing or paying attention to what you have, then ruminato (ruminating) on what you want to accomplish. What is this ruminato? Ruminato is from the Latin word ruminare, meaning "I chew the cud." The English word ruminate stems from its root word ruminant, which is a mammal, such as a sheep or goat, that chews it's cud. So cud chewing is a conformity allowing ruminants to graze more quickly earlier in the day and then fully chew and digest feed later in the day. This is safer than grazing, that requires ruminants to lower their head while eating thus leaving the animal vulnerable to predators. Cud chewing allows the mammals to be diligent about it's eating while knowing the condition of it's safety. The definition of ruminate is; chewing the cud, to chew over and over, to mull or go over, or to meditate on something. To mull over or go over or even meditate on the situation which you have concern. Buyah! Meditate over and over on your financial situation. Now, when you know or have paid attention to your situation, you meditate on it. And when you have meditated on it long enough, then you seek to find a solution, you come up with a plan. W. L. Bateman said, "If you keep on doing what you've always done, you'll keep on getting what you've always got." Time to change what we are doing. That is why the bible says in Romans 12:2(NKJV) *"And do not be conformed to this world, but be transformed by the renewing of your mind, that you may prove what is that good and acceptable and perfect will of God."*

One day when we were eyebrow deep in debt, struggling to make it to the next pay check (like 70% of American families), hoping that there were no financial setbacks that pay period, feeling house poor (paying too much mortgage for the house we were living in), my wife, being stressed out over our situation, came to me and said I needed to do something or she was gone. She saw in me someone who was in a financial mess and really wasn't doing much to change it. I must admit that I was aware of our failing-scrawny flocks and herds, but saw no need to go to code red. You recall, I had grown up financially stressed (yes poor), and could easily tolerate a much lesser lifestyle. My wife did not share the same up-bringings, there-in was one of our differences. Two different up-bringing, two different financial perspectives. I was not crazy about our debt, but I knew I would always make enough to eventually pay it off. I had ruminated enough on our situation to know I had made so many bad financial decisions and still somehow, didn't think it was that bad. I now imagine it was like Lieutenant Colonel George Armstrong Custer, telling his men at the Battle of the Little Bighorn, "there's a lot of Indians out there, but it's not that bad." As I ruminated, I saw the unraveling of our family's flocks and herds (finances) and could hear my wife's voice telling me I needed to do something. At the time, I had so many other things going on in my life that were so demanding; my job, several ministries at church, the family, the house, the honey do list (which was getting longer every time I turned around) and of course "life" was going on in my life. I subsequently found myself in the state of "flux." The state of flux is a state of uncertainty about what should be done (usually following the happening of some important event) preceding the establishment of a new direction of action (as defined by thefreedictionary.com); the flux following the demise of our flocks and herds. I did not want a new financial direction. I was willing to modify my existing financial strategies. The flocks and herds weren't all dead, yet. Was it the paralysis of analysis? Was it pride? Was it the shame of "I told you so" from my wife? Or was it the failure of the desire to do needed change - change from the ways this world had taught me? I thought - I can still fix it. I have learned that much of our decisions (financial or otherwise) are based on our family, friends, upbringing, life experiences, education (even cheap books), and other factors. In essence, this world has taught our minds to be conformed to principles which impacts us greatly in our decision making. My wife said I needed to do something, I was doing something, but that something was not working.

 According to the distractify.com, the life expectancy in America is 78.6 years. What financial goals would I accomplish in my 78 years and how would I spend my time reaching them? I thought this was funny. The average

American spends 25 years sleeping, 13.2 years working, 9.1 years watching television, 2 years watching commercials. Do you think watching commercials have anything to do with women spending 8 years shopping? The average American spends 14 days kissing and 48 days having sex. I put that in to wake some of you up. Also, shouldn't those numbers be reversed? In addition, men spend one year staring at women, I only mentioned that because women spend one year deciding what to wear and 1.5 years doing their hair. I did not research it, I am just reporting it. Finally, the average American spends 1.5 years in the bathroom, at least take this book with you, it shouldn't take that long to read. Do you think that in 9.1 years of television and countless commercials and subtle messages, that our decision making could be influenced? Just to show you how subtle this conformity works, finish this statement. "What's in your ____?" Capital One. You might be smart enough to ignore those subtle messages, but the constant barrage of similar messages just might affect your financial decision making. That is why we should not be conformed to this world, but be transformed by the renewing of your mind. I try to spend the first hour of my day praying and in God's Word and the second hour, watching the liberal news. That way, I know what both sides are doing. When we use God's Word to guide us in our decision making, we usually end up in God's Will. When we use the world's influence to guide us in our decision making, we usually end up outside of God's Will and in debt. It is amazing how I can read a scripture, commit it to memory, forget that it existed (even in a crisis) and God brings it back to memory at the right time. Romans 12:2(NKJV) was one such scripture, *"And do not be conformed to this world, but be transformed by the renewing of your mind, that you may prove what is that good and acceptable and perfect will of God."* When we take this scripture to heart, it is one of the most powerful verses in the Bible. The Bible was telling me not to be in agreement with or have similar character with the ways of this world, that I had to wipe out the old hard drive and replace it with God's Will in my life. For the computer geeks, I had to reboot myself. I, like many other Christian believers, struggled through life with various bondages; depression, selfishness, drug and sex addictions, finances, failure, etc. Christians see their failures as a weakness they cannot overcome while some blame others and sometimes God for their misfortunes. Reboot: *"Misfortune pursues sinners, but prosperity is the reward of the righteous,"* (Proverbs 13:21 (NIV)). Reboot: *"God has made us more than conquerors,"* (Romans 8:37(NKJV)). Reboot: *"because greater is he that is in us, than he who is in the world,"* (1John 4:4(KJV)). When our minds are renewed to the Word of God, we will be overcomers, conquerors of the bondages in our lives, allowing us to live a life that is good and acceptable and in the perfect will of God.

Many Christians struggle through life in financial bondage and scratch their heads trying to figure out why they are having problems. Some even search the scriptures in order to support their financial bondage life style. Reasoning that scriptures like: *"Give to him who asks of you, and do not turn away from him who wants to borrow from you,"* (Matthew 5:42(NKJV)); or *"But when you give to the poor, do not let your left hand know what your right hand is doing,"* (Matthew 6:3, New American Standard Bible (NASB)); When Jesus encountered a rich young ruler who inquired about enternal life, ultimately *"Jesus said to him, If you wish to be [a]complete, go and sell your possessions and give to the poor, and you will have treasure in heaven; and come, follow Me,"* (Matthew 19:21(NASB)). So, some of us don't have because we have interpreted the scriptures to say that God has told us to give it all away, or God has asked us to give our wealth to the poor, or that we must have little possessions to keep ourselves humbled. Listen, *"But if anyone does not provide for his own, and especially for those of his household, he has denied the faith and is worse than an unbeliever"* (1 Timothy 5:8(NASB)). Even those of you who are believers in Christ, are in agreement of this supposed contradiction of the scriptures. If you are a believer, but are not taking care of your family, then you are worse than the unbeliever. Now the unbelievers are seeing scriptures that say that there are believers who are worse than them. Wow, that's different.

Look, let us not go into supersonic theology, ruminate on this. *"Will a man rob God? Yet you have robbed Me! But you say, "In what way have we robbed You?" In tithes and offerings. You are cursed with a curse For, you have robbed Me, Even this whole nation. Bring all the tithes into the storehouse, that there may be food in My house, and try Me now in this, Says the Lord of hosts, If I will not open for you the windows of heaven and pour out for you such blessing That there will not be room enough to receive it,"* Malachi 3:8(NKJV). Give to God first and you can't go wrong. In fact, God challenges you with a blessing that you cannot contain. God is not only daring you, He is double dog daring you to bring your tithes to the house of God. I don't know about you, but I would take him up on the dare. Your first financial responsibility is to God and secondly to your family. But, for those who say I am disobeying what Jesus said because I am not giving all I have to the poor, look at this. The Bible says that if you owe a man and have it within your means to pay him but don't, you are wicked. Therefore, if you have created a debt, whether it be a gas or electric bill, rent or mortgage, a credit card bill or personal debt, you are obligated to pay off that debt before giving to the poor, the less fortunate, your broke brother-n-law, or church friend to keep their cable on. Some of us have gotten into trouble by creating debt so we can have money to give to the poor. Even worse, putting gifts to the poor and needy on our credit cards. Jesus said the poor you have with you always. Some are trying to make Jesus a liar by trying to ensure that everyone has stuff that they did not work for; a house, they cannot afford; or a car, they cannot take care of. My wife says that Dave Ramsey's budget is correctly assembled. Giving and saving is done at the top of the budget and not at the bottom. God and the Banks family got paid first. For so many years, we set up our budget to pay others before we pay God and ourselves. More about the dreaded "B" word later.

To be transformed is to go through a complete change. I am still transforming (my wife is thankful for that). There are still parts of me that tends toward the worldly way of doing finances. Having one credit card (that is paid off monthly) isn't that bad. That borrowing money to start up a business (using someone else money) isn't that bad. That financing a car because everybody has a car payment (even at 0% interest) isn't that bad. Or not giving every dollar a name or knowing well the condition of my flocks or being attentive to my herds. Then the scripture comes back to me, *"The rich rules over the poor and the borrower is a slave to the lender,"* (Proverbs 22:7(NKJV)). Going from a big debt to a small debt, from 10 credit cards to 3 credit cards, from no budget to an ignored budget are not transformations. The Greek word for transformed is "metamorpho." It defines the change that a caterpillar goes through when it comes out of it's cocoon as a beautiful butterfly. It's going from a big debt to no debt, from 10 credit cards to 0 credit cards, from no budget to a living budget, from negligence to knowing well and being attentive. Those are transformations.

We come to church every week to learn something new, what thus said the Lord, having our soul stirred as the preacher brought the "Worrrdtha of Goddda." The sermon, to say the least, was uplifting, invigorating, stimulating and moving; but did we ever really consider changing the way we thought or lived? Not only do we not make decisions to change, we don't even think about changing. It reminds me of a story I once heard about a pastor who took over church. He was excited and the congregation, which had been without a pastor for a while, was also excited. The pastor preached his first sermon and the "Worrrdtha of Goddda" came forth with great oratory skill. The congregation told the pastor his sermon was uplifting, invigorating, stimulating and moving. The second Sunday came around and the pastor was excited and likewise the congregation. The pastor preached the same "Worrrdtha of Goddda" message. The congregation was somewhat puzzled, but told the pastor his sermon was uplifting, invigorating and stimulating. So, the third Sunday came around and the pastor preached the same "Worrrdtha of Goddda" message. Now, the congregation was beginning to get concerned, but told the pastor his sermon was uplifting and invigorating. When the fourth Sunday came around and the pastor had preached the same message, the congregation began to think that the pastor was senile, but told the pastor his sermon was uplifting. When the same thing happened a fifth time, the congregation approached the pastor and told him his sermons were uplifting, invigorating, stimulating and moving, and asked him when he going to change his message. The Pastor told the congregation, "when you tell me the sermons are changing you, then I will change my sermon."

    My wife and I were talking about our finances and the need of having our minds renewed. She said for her, knowing that all the gold and silver belongs to the Lord was pivoting in the renewing of her mind. For her, knowing that it all belongs to God, it took away some of the financial pressures of it being all on us. She says it all belongs to him so why should we worry about someone else's money. It is not like all the money is in the hands of our Aunt Screwloose or Uncle Knutbrain. God owns it and knows what He is doing with it. We on the other hand, that's a different story. She says now, when she sees money, she thinks differently about it, understanding that God probably has a plan and a purpose for His money. She is trying to become aware of His financial purpose in her life. I told her my thoughts of having a renewed mind, that I thought of stewardship. Before becoming aware of what I thought about our finances, I thought I was doing "my part." However, once I understood that God's thoughts were way different than my thoughts, I recognized my need of a renewing. It meant that I had to practice those (God) thoughts until they became actions in my everyday life. Before a renewing of my mind, when I got paid, I gave God his part (tithes and offerings) and I got my part (what was used to pay bills and support family). God's good, I'm good, family good, bills good, "all God's chillens good." But my wife and this Dave Ramsey book began to - I am going old school on this - pester me. When I was a child living in rural Texas, I would get a long stick and poke at my Big Momma's (Grandmother's) dog. The dog was named "Three" (because he only had three legs). While lying there in that hot Texas sun, Three would first growl at the stick and then bite it. Eventually, Three would get up chase me and I would drop the stick and run. My Big Momma would say, "boy, stop pestering that dog before he bites you." That is how I felt, like Three, pestered. Those scriptures on stewardship kept pestering me until I got up and did something about it.

In "Taking Care of Business," by Lee Jenkins, he writes, "Christian stewardship begins with the understanding that all we have belongs to God, that He has made us stewards, or managers, of his possessions and that the Lord will reward us according to the actions and the attitudes of our stewardship." In Luke 12:42-44(NKJV), the bible says *"And the Lord said, who then is that faithful and wise steward, whom his master will make ruler over his household, to give them their portion of food in due season? Blessed is that servant whom his master will find so doing when he comes. Truly, I say to you that he will make him ruler over all that* he has." The bible also talks about an unjust steward in Luke 16:1-3(NKJV); *"He also said to His disciples: There was a certain rich man who had a steward, and an accusation was brought to him that this man was wasting his goods. He called him and said to him, What is this I hear about you? Give an account of your stewardship, for you can no longer be steward. Then the steward said within himself, what shall I do? For my master is taking the stewardship away from me. I cannot dig; I am ashamed to beg."* I had to ask myself, was I being a faithful and wise steward or an unjust steward? Was there more that I should be doing with God's money? Yes.

According to Casey Treat, Author of "Renewing the Mind," renewing the mind is so much more than going through religious motions. It is a conscious effort and labor to:

1. Become aware of how we really think and believe,
2. Become aware of how God wants us to think,
3. Focus our thoughts on God thoughts,
4. Practice the thoughts of God until they are our own, and
5. Live the thoughts of God with our actions in everyday life.

REFLECTIONS

Now that you know that you should know the state your finances, will you set up several days a month to review your banking accounts?

Will you schedule a consultation with a certified financial planner? The first consultation is usually free

FRUGAL

In the house of the righteous there is much treasure, but trouble befalls the income of the wicked. Proverbs 15:6(RSV)

Going back to a story I previously told, in 1997, the pastor of the Apostolic Faith Church, Kenosha, WI, allowed me to teach finances during a Wednesday night service. I told of several methods of saving money. The congregation, like most, seemed less than enthusiastic about the subject of budgeting their finances. I really couldn't blame them because one of the money saving methods I shared was the reusing of paper towels in the members households. Of course, this met with some snickering and comments. Now I should have come up with something better than that one. Almost twenty years later, we still reuse some of the used paper towels at our home. The other day I came across this bit of information; the average household uses 1 to 2 rolls of paper towels a week (not if you have teenagers) and at about $10 for two 4-packs, you could be spending up $120 - $180 a year for that convenience. Now if a person reused 25-30% of a roll of paper towels, that is two rolls saved out of an 8-pack, equating to $2.25 - $3.25. Which then extrapolates to about $45.00 a year. In 10 years, that is a new flat screen TV, I'm just saying. I know, I should have left it out of this book. But the bible says, *"Do not despise these small beginnings, for the Lord rejoices to see the work begin, to see the plumb line in Zerubbabel's hand,"* (Zech 4:10 (The Living Bible(TLB)). Maybe not the results you had in mind, but it is a start to the frugality process. Or what I like to call it, the wise ways to wealth. This is not cheap. You see cheap, by definition, ranges from things low in price or inexpensive to stingy, low, vulgar or contemptible. Frugality differs in that it is economical in use or expenditure; prudently saving or sparing; not wasteful: I think that the wise ways to wealth is the due diligence to first know the condition of your flocks, research your options, and finally become the best steward you can be.

Here are some wise ways to wealth that we did to help save monies in our budget, that just might help your budget. Understand these are temporary adjustments until you get your budget where you need it to be. TEMPORARY (And they are better than the paper towels story):

1. Prayer: I know that sounds "super spiritual," but it isn't. It was humbling ourselves and asking God for knowledge, wisdom, and divine favor with our finances. Besides, it was part of our budget that didn't financially cost anything, but time.
2. Savings: We used what little savings we had to pay off one bill. That freed up $309 a month in our budget. We set up several savings accounts for major components of our budget such as our emergency fund, a sinking fund, a car and vacation fund, and a fund for each one of our children, that they don't know about(so don't tell them).
3. Mortgage: We refinanced our mortgage and lowered our monthly payment. That added about $127 to our budget. By refinancing, we met at least 20% equity in the home and terminated the PMI. We saved another $67 a month.

4. Real Estate Taxes: After refinancing, we optioned out of our escrow. We paid our mortgage company principal and interest payments. Our real estate and insurance payments were paid by us at the end of the year. We controlled the money and we kept any interest made on the money. We researched the county's real estate tax assessor's appraisal of our home and compared with other compatible home values in our community. We protested the appraisal and had it reduced.
5. Home Operations: We did our own lawn service. We only watered the lawn twice a week. We did our own pest control. We did our own minor carpentry, plumbing and electrical repairs. In Texas, on 100 degree days, we set our thermostat at 78 degrees. We closed HVAC vents and shut doors to rooms not used. We turned off lights that were not being used. We terminated our land-line phone and only used cell phones. We rented the equipment, and cleaned our own carpet. Every year, we shopped for a better cable deal. One time, I recall getting on the roof and installing a satellite dish. We never used "Pay for Review" and premium channels. We replaced appliances ourselves and never bought the extended warranties. When we bought appliances, we shopped the "scratch and dent" and "clearance" sections first. In fact, "Clearance" became our family's best friend, and not just with appliances. We shopped for clothing in the clearance section. It sometime takes extra effort, but you can put outfits together from the clearance racks. We ate out less, therefore we had to terminate the after-church dinners with our friends. I know, call me a back-slider. Some of us can't/don't pay tithes, but by God, we are first in line at the buffet, all in the name of "Fellowshipping." Sounds more like "Meals Mission." Sorry, I got side tracked. Since we ate out less, we had to shop for

groceries in a wiser manner. Grocery shopping tips: 1; Don't go to the grocery store hungry. 2; Have a list. 3; Leave children and spouse at home. Every time I went to the store with my wife, she said it cost us more money. That's because I grew up without much food and I made a promise that my children would always have food to eat. My wife was kind of ok with that, but she had a problem with me trying to buy up the entire store (because the store was not in our budget). We clipped coupons, bought generic brands (if generic is a brand), bought bulk when feasible, and used in store specials. We even planted gardens and fruit trees in our back yards.

6. Insurance: I had been paying for our life insurance via my government job. The policy covered me (several hundred thousand dollars), my wife ($5,000) and children ($2,500 each). I canceled our government policy, except for the basic policy on me and after shopping around, increased my wife's policy to $200,000 and children's riders for $25,000. Two of our children were in college during our financial woes and were part of our government health plan. When they turned 26, they were removed from our plan and we bought them an emergency health plan for about a $100 a month. Not great, but better than a poke in the eye with a sharp stick.

7. Vehicles: We had three vehicles, we were making car payments on one of them. As I wrote earlier, we were frugal and thrifty and paid that one off. We only bought cash cars ($1,500 - $3,000) during our financial struggle. No monthly car payments. When buying a cash car, remember, these are your finances, you stay in control. Don't let the salesperson dictate the terms. God put his money into your hands. Tell the salesperson you like the car, but you need to look

around and that you will be back. You will get a better deal or you wont be back. When our 1991 Volvo was totaled, it was still operable. We took a lesser check (by $150) from the insurance company and kept the vehicle. Then we canceled the collision policy on the vehicle. I conducted many of the routine maintenance and minor repairs. I bought tires as needed and not an entire set. Knowing that an entire set of tires would have greatly impacted our budget. We used the cheapest rated fuel for our cars.

8. Health: I was going to mention this in the food section but thought health could use its own section. I have never been a fan of paying to work out. Now my thinking is this, if I was paying a health club, "Betcha By Golly Wow" (The Stylistics, 1975), I am going to be there to work out. Why? Because I paid God's money. However, go to the gym in April and attendance in April or May is down from January. Why? Because it's not always about the money, it about behavior (commitment and discipline). Here's a thought, put your professional body building agenda on the side burner for a short while and put that money back into your budget. Instead, get up and walk in the morning. If you are married, discuss the Bible or the agenda for the day. Get on the same page with your finances. How about, a budget walking meeting or work out at your church. What, you don't have a workout ministry at your church? Then start one. Here is another one; your children are on that expensive select sports team. Take them off and put that money back into your budget. What are they going to do? You can work that out with them. Can you throw, hit or kick a ball? If they maintain that desire to play that sport and not because you desire that they play sports, then you will see their eagerness to return to it, when the family can afford it. I realize I am on

borderline blasphemy here, but if your child is gifted in an area, the Bible says their gift will make room for them. Eat better, less can goods are always better. Fresh fruits and vegetables are healthier, therefore hopefully, less medical bills. If you are diagnosed with an illness, "Google" it. You might find different and better ways to treat the illness, perhaps even less expensive ways. If it is major, get a second opinion. Speaking of second opinions, we searched for doctors who practiced preventive care. When we bought over-the-counter medicines, we compared ingredients with the named brands and purchased the less expensive medications.

9. Miscellaneous: We cut our children's hair until they got jobs and paid for their own. My wife braided, straightened, put in relaxers, etc., in our daughter's hair. I put relaxers and dyed my wife's hair. Now brother-man, four things I must share with you about processing your wife's hair: 1) Pray before you start. Your wife sees that you care enough about what you are doing to call upon the Lord. If things go bad, she will grant you mercy and spare your life.; 2) Never do your wife's hair while your favorite team is on TV. If things go bad, she will not grant you mercy and will not spare your life.; 3) Regardless how things go, tell her she looks "modern" and great. I don't know what modern means, but as she ponders, it will give you time to escape.; and 4) Keep doing her hair as long as she will allow it. You will get better and she will trust you and love you more. We stopped buying clothing. We had enough clothes in our closet to keep us for a while. We home schooled our children (not for financial reasons, but it did save us money). There are free tutorials for children who are struggling in certain subjects. We bought used reading books for our

children. We took our children to the public library to research their school work. When our children got part time jobs, we had them give to the church, the house budget, save and spend for themselves. I packed dinner left overs for my lunch (except when we had fish). We had designated days for clothes to be washed and yard to be watered to help control water usage.

10. Finance: First, we had to, "Know well the condition of your flocks, be attentive to your herds." Therefore, we had to find out what were our finances, after seeing what we were working with, we did a budget, then a plan to get out of debt. We both took the Dave Ramsey Financial Peace University class. We visited a financial planner. We started a plan to save $1000 emergency fund. We stopped creating debt. We cut up our credit cards. Cut down on out-going cash gifts and give aways. We worked part time. We operated with cash envelopes for gas, food, entertainment, commission and miscellaneous. We had timely financial meetings between the two of us. We opened several other savings accounts; vehicle, vacation, emergency and sinking funds. We used automatic withdrawal to fund several of the saving accounts. After becoming debt free, we set a fixed amount that was invested. We both started Roth IRAs. We started several home-based businesses to make extra money and increased our tax deductions. We bought and flipped (slow rolled) a house. We opened accounts at several banks to accomplish our goals. We utilized silver (old folks) accounts that did not charge fees. When we could help others, we did by giving to them and not loaning out money. We lived on the plan. Then we lived on the plan, and when we did not want to, we lived on the plan.

In an U.S. News & World Report article, "5 Rewards of Living a Frugal Lifestyle," by Kassandra Dasent, she said, "You might be a natural at making frugal choices when it comes to spending or perhaps you are slowly easing your way into the frugal lifestyle. Either way, know that your efforts result in additional benefits that go beyond the immediate impact of cash savings. You might not notice these non-monetary rewards at first. That's because in the beginning stages of adopting a frugal perspective, you're usually focused on reaping the primary benefit, which is saving money. What I have discovered and what many others report, is that living frugally encourages a heightened level of awareness. Here are five positive rewards that can be obtained resulting from your commitment to minding your money: Improved health - less stress and more sleep, Better relationships – when both parties are on the same page financially, they have fewer arguments, Greater appreciation – for the things you have because you buy less, A sense of accomplishment – meeting financial goals and saving money, and Financial security – being out of debt, setting up an emergency fund or investing in your retirement account."

Using frugality as part of our stewardship make-up, helps us to keep more cents and dollars in our budget. This helps us to establish an emergency fund, eliminate debt, be able to afford funding our retirement goals, putting in place our children college education, building wealth and helping family and others. Let us use frugality as a method in proper stewardship and not have a spirit of frugality. When I was called a kuripot (cheapskate) in the Philippines, I was proud of myself for arguing with the store keeper. God checked me and had me look at my spirit. I was developing a spirit (attitude) of frugality and not kindness to my fellow man. "Huwag kang kuripot," means don't be a cheapskate. Cents and dollars over time adds up to freedom and wealth. Frugality is characterized by using wisdom in the use of your God given resources. It is not like one person who collected rice after it was thrown at a wedding and cooking it for dinner. That is "stupality," meaning stupid frugality. Don't bother Webster, it is not there.

REFLECTIONS

Do you think that all prices are final?

When was the last time you asked for a lower cost on an items?

Are you scared of the word NO?

Guess what, you also have the power of NO.

TIME TO GO
(And visit your flocks and herds)

In the first chapter of this book, I wrote about our family moving from Texas to Ohio. In 1965, my single Mother and her seven children left all we had; family, broken furniture, house without a bathtub, poor conditions, no public assistance, no car, we didn't even have a phone. I look back on her decision and marvel at her courage to let go of her known and move to the unknown. After all, Texas was all she knew and was all she had. She knew it was not great, but she had accepted it and lived with it for years. Why let go and move? Because sometimes, it's just time to go.

I came across a story about how monkey hunters in India carry out their task. The monkey hunter cuts a small hole in one end of a coconut, just large enough for a monkey's hand to fit inside of the coconut. Next, the monkey hunter ties a long cord to the other end of the coconut. Then he places an enticing treat like banana pieces or peanuts inside of the coconut. The monkey hunter places the coconut in a place where an unsuspecting monkey will smell the treat and the hunter takes the cord in hand and hides. Inevitably, an monkey comes along, smells the treat, sticks his hand into the coconut to retrieve the delicacy and bam!, the hunter has his catch. All the hunter needs to do is to pull in the monkey. Once the monkey closes his hand around the treat inside the coconut, his fist is too large to pass back through the hole and he wouldn't open his hand and let go. If the monkey would only let go in his situation, he would save his life. Understand that some of us need to let go of the life we are living and save ourselves. We need to let go and let God. We need to let go of our poor financial decisions and let God help us with financial wisdom. We have found ourselves in financially stressed, debt incurred, spending frenzy, friend funding, buddy begging, family financing and a money managing mess. One of the strangest things is that many of us are OK and have even become comfortable in our money messes. Like our mother, she decided to let go of Texas, her comfort, and move to the never charted land of Ohio. Now that I look back at her decision, what did she have to lose. Poor and hungry is poor and hungry, no matter what state you are in. Guess what, when we got to Ohio, I thought our rich uncle had gotten out of the poor house. We rented a brick house with heat and window panes, we were living high on the hog. That move opened-up opportunities for me and our family which were next to impossible in Texas. In high school, I received National Honor Society accolades and was the first to graduate from college in my family. Likewise, my siblings did better. Many opportunities were obtained because my mother decided to let go of what we had and reach for something better. Beverly Sills (BrainyQuote) said: There are no shortcuts to any place worth going."

My friend, we are at that time, time to go. It is time to go back and utilize wisdom from the old school. To know well the condition of our flocks and be attentive to our herds. Being attentive is to do something with or about: the way we do our finances. Some of you are not seeing my mother's experience in connections with their finances, but it was about finances. Just like it is about flocks and herds. It was my mother having or getting the finances to help her and her seven kids survive. It is you having or getting the finances you need to help you and your family to survive. It's being obedient to a calling to which you know not the journey nor the ending. It's like Abraham in the 11th and 12th chapters in the book of Genesis NKJV (11:31- 12:5). *"And Terah took his son Abram and his grandson Lot, the son of Haran, and his daughter-in-law Sarai, his son Abram's wife, and they went out with them from Ur of the Chaldeans to go to the land of Canaan; and they came to Haran and dwelt there. So, the days of Terah were two hundred and five years, and Terah died in Haran." Now the Lord had said to Abram: "Get out of your country, from your family and from your father's house, to a land that I will show you. I will make you a great nation; I will bless you and make your name great; And you shall be a blessing. I will bless those who bless you, and I will curse him who curses you; And in you all the families of the earth shall be blessed. So, Abram departed as the Lord had spoken to him, and Lot went with him. And Abram was seventy-five years old when he departed from Haran. Then Abram took Sarai his wife, Lot his brother's son, and all their possessions that they had gathered, and the people whom they had acquired in Haran, and they departed to go to the land of Canaan. So, they came to the land of Canaan."* And in chapter 13:1-4(NKJV): *"Then Abram went up from Egypt, he and his wife and all that he had, and Lot with him, to the South. Abram was very rich in livestock, in silver, and in gold. And he went on his journey from the South as far as Bethel, to the place where his tent had been at the beginning, between Bethel and Ai, to the place of the altar which he had made there at first. And there Abram called on the name of the Lord."*

Lot also, who went with Abram, had flocks and herds and tents. Now the land was not able to support them, that they might dwell together, for their possessions were so great that they could not dwell together. Abram and Lot left Heran with their meager flocks and herds. By the time Abram and Lot arrived at Bethel a second time, where Abram had previously built an alter, their flocks and herds had grown to make them very rich. It's amazing what happens when we know well the condition of our flocks and be attentive to our herds (when we know the condition of our finances and put in motion our currency). Abram was obedient to God and prospered. I am not saying for you to literally move from your physical location, well unless where you live is detrimental to your lively hood, but more of a move of your cerebral thought position. What I am suggesting is that if your flocks and herds are weak and not as healthy as you want them to be, then move. One of the shepherd's duties is to change grazing pastures of the flocks and herds. If left in one place too long, the food supply will become depleted and the livestock will suffer from the lack. The shepherd's change in pastures, while sometimes difficult, is best for his flocks. Change or move from the way you think and treat your finances. Bruce Barton (author) said "When you're through changing, you're through." If it is your desire to have a better financial year and you are willing to move from your present financial position, then this is your year. Proverbs 13:12 (NKJV) says *"Hope deferred makes the heart sick, but when the desire comes, it is a tree of life."* When your desire for financial freedom is met, you will have life and joy.

Confession time, I am a procrastinator. My wife had been trying to get me to enroll into some type of financial class for years. I kept putting it off by telling her I would as soon as I got a break in my job. Or when my church scheduled lessons. The truth was I did not think that we were in that bad of a financial situation. While at the same time, our finances were killing our relationship and our marriage. Then I really messed up and told my wife about a Dave Ramsey's Financial Peace University class being given at my work associate's church. My wife jumped at the opportunity to attend, but there was another problem, the class was on Monday nights (during football season). So, when she suggested we go, I thought she had been smoking something with a funny odor. Despite my pleas to take the next available class, I went complaining and fussing. Proverb 10:4 (NKJV) *"He who has a slack hand becomes poor, But the hand of the diligent makes rich."* Ted's translation, procrastination keeps you poor, but those who do rich people stuff, they become rich. The Bible uses words like lazy, slothful, sluggard, slack, etc. I throw the word procrastinator into that group. Someone who puts off taking action, procrastinates. The book of Proverbs says the lazy man won't even lift his hand to put bread in his mouth or cook his prey after catching it. Proverbs 20:4 (KJV): *"The sluggard will not plow by reason of the cold; therefore, shall he beg in harvest, and have nothing."* A procrastinator's flocks and herds are going to be weak, feeble and in need of attention. A quote from a John Maxwell, "A procrastinator puts off until tomorrow the things he has already put off until today." James Michener said, "Don't put off for tomorrow what you can do today, because if you enjoy it today, you can do it again tomorrow."

Robb Thompson, "What God Thinks About Money," said "The moment we make a decision is the moment we have determined our success or failure." Deuteronomy 30:19 (NKJV), says *"I call heaven and earth as witnesses today against you, that I have set before you, life and death, blessing and cursing; therefore, choose life, that both you and your descendants may live;"* In fact, if you look at Deuteronomy 28:1-14 (NKJV), you will see God's Blessing (many financial) on His people, because of their obedience. God promised Joshua prosperity and success for his obedience to the written Word. Proverbs say it is a fool who despises wisdom and instruction. Just remember, one of our biggest financial mistakes has been to ignore our finances. Or like many of the characters in the Bible who did not ignore their situation and change their minds: Jacob, when he wrestled with the divine being, Jonah in the fish belly, Saul (later Paul) when he was blinded, etc.

Hopefully, your finances are not in dire straight, but if they are, don't wait until disaster hits to move you to be attentive to your flocks and herds. Let's go! It's time to be attentive to your finances and get them moving now.

So to all, it's time to go.

REFLECTIONS

Now that you know and are ready to go, what is your next move?

Do you have a short term (less than five years) and a long term (greater than five years) financial plan?

WHAT TO DO/ HOW WE DID IT

The plans of the diligent lead surely to plenty, but those of everyone who is hasty, surely to poverty
Proverbs 21:5 (NKJV)

We paid off over $94,000 in three and one-half years. That's not mentioning the additional $473,000 in three mortgages (2003-2006). After we read Total Money Makeover by Dave Ramsey in 2006, we began by examining our finances. Let me reiterate, "Know well the condition of your flocks, and give attention to your herds." I know, I know, you've heard that before. Anyway, we began to make a plan to pay off something, then pay off everything. Then in 2008 we took Dave's Financial Peace University course and made a commitment to stay the course of his seven baby steps to financial freedom.

Listening to my wife reading the Total Money Makeover as we drove to California, was kinda like a prisoner watching a movie. The movie might be great, but when you wake up in the morning, you are still in prison. As my wife was reading, I was counting down the miles on the slow passing mile posts markers to California. When we reached El Paso, Texas, I remembered someone saying that El Paso was closer to Los

Know Well (Wealth) Your Flocks and Herds

Angeles than it was to Dallas. I was saying to myself that's crazy on one side of my brain and listen to words from Dave about living like no one else so later you can live like no one else and saying to myself (on the other side of my brain) that's crazy. Of course, I know the sisterhood is saying that is impossible, because the brotherhood cannot utilize both sides of his brain at once. This stuff about baby steps, money myths, paying off debt and not having credit cards, that is crazy. So, on the return trip from visiting California, I think we were somewhere in Way-West Texas, when my wife finished the Total Money Makeover, she closed the book and the moment of dread came. The mile posts seemed to pass in slow motion. She politely smiled and asked the question "So what do you think?" Translation, now, what are you going to do about our debt, you lazy sluggard? Just like a horror movie, all the viewers know the monster is hiding in the bushes except the poor slob who is about to become a Monster Happy Meal. I did my normal long silent response. Now, I don't want any of you to think that all of that reading fell on deaf ears. Maybe I did not listen to or even understand all of Dave's words, but I did understand two things; First, in order to change our financial future, I had to be willing to change what I was doing today and secondly, I would do whatever it took to save our marriage. Therefore, I gave the response most husbands would give, "Well, I don't know, what do you think?" She responded, "You already know what I think," (which I did) "I want to know what you think." "Well," I started out again, knowing I was about to become that Monster Happy Meal, "I think we, we, should, uhh, get out of debt." Wow, I had said it. It was like confessing my sins. I think the sun shined brighter, the birds sang prettier and the mile posts zipped by like a blur. Relief right. No, my wife pushed. "Well how?" she said. Oh no, she stole my line, I had to start my response with something else. "Uhh" was about the best I could do at the time. Then I said, when we return home, we will look at our finances and determine how we should proceed. She seemed happily-skeptical.

Let me say something about what Dave Ramsey did to me in the Total Money Makeover. He hit me with a "denial" upper-cut, a "debt is not a tool" jab and a "money myth" haymaker that knocked me out. I stood up from the ten count, I realized that what people like Dave Ramsey, Ron Blu, Larry Burkett and others wanted for me was to have a financial plan. Well by all my understanding, I had a financial plan. Like most Americans, we have financial plans, however my plan (like many) was small, weak, unenforced and unwritten. When people asked me if I had a budget, I would jokingly pat my hand on my pants pocket and say "yeah, it's right here." Or they would ask if it was written down and I would point to my head and say "yeah, it's right here." My wife suggested that I not point to my head, insinuating that I had a brain. My financial plan was so small at times, not even I could see it. My wife had a plan and I couldn't see hers. Not because it was too small, but because I could not see living off dust and walking to work (18.5 miles) just to get out of debt. But what Dave offered was a "SEVEN BABY-STEP PLAN" that was big enough, we could both see it and it was written down in plain language. *"And the Lord answered me: Write the vision; make it plain upon tablets, so he may run who reads it,* "Habakkuk 2:2(RSV).

Now, when we returned home we began to run with the process. Man-o-man, we did budgets. Well I had a budget and my wife had a budget and we tried adding the two together. That doubled our woes and those combined budgets did not work. Then we tried joining, augmenting, annexing, affixing, tacking on, adding on, piling on, summing on, on-n-on and so on. It was not until we both sat down together in unity with a simple conventional budget outline and came up with a unified plan supported by both of our input and backed by both of our finances, were we successful? Yes, because all our finances were on the kitchen table. Not part of one of our finances, not some keeping some of it in a tea pot, metal can or under the mattress. All the money on the table in one bundle with no one's name on it, but what we called "house money."

With a budget, we discovered the places where all our house money was going. Some places; bills, charities, tithes and offering are good, and some places; credit cards, excessive cable bill, high cell phone costs and restaurants can be bad places for money when we were financially struggling. After plugging our finances into the budget, we also saw the leaks and crevices in our finances. Just like the shepherd who arises in the morning and counts his flock and finds one of his precious lambs missing. That shepherd seeks to find out what happened to the little lamb and how to prevent that from happening again. We sought not only to find out what happened to our house money but also to adjust our budget to prevent wasteful spending and to use wise discretion. Now it was not a one-shot effort with our budget, but many efforts to get it somewhat right. Then the month we got it right, we had to do another budget the next month and every month afterward. The more we did our budgets, the easier they became to do. Fewer disagreements and more control over our finances. We saw that by controlling our finances, telling our money where to go, it seemed we had gotten a raise in our salaries. Not only did we experience this, others have told us the same thing. When you control your money, you are empowered and often will find money that you did not know you had. We began to see the possibility of our plan of being debt free come to fruition, if we kept our budget plan enforced.

Now as bad as our finances were we did have a little savings of about $4,000. See, I am not a total looser. We immediately removed $1,000 from our savings, opened a money market account, deposited the money and took care of the first step of Dave Ramsey, Financial Peace University (FPU). That felt pretty good and the wife was happy. For some of you, getting $1,000 seems like an impossibility, but it's not. Easy for you to say Ted Banks, you had $4,000. True, but how many of you are starting out their journey in over $400,000 of debt (including two mortgages). About $86,000 of that debt were a vehicle and a personal loan, credit cards and line of credit debt and living life. You see in the mist of our debt crisis, I had a great idea. I bought a small house for $87,000 and planned to repair and flip it. After all, not only had my son and I had gone to one of those "free" real estate seminar, which we then paid $1,000 for a weekend class to prepare us for that prosperous journey into entrepreneurial house flipping mega-bucks. Now, I understand why Dave Ramsey says to buy real estate with cash. The house flipping class not only encouraged credit card usage, the class taught participants to contact their banks and get a credit limit increased on their existing cards. I did that and was encouraged to get additional credit cards to finance my house flipping endeavors. Plus, I did not think it necessary to tell my wife about the extra four credit cards I obtained. Well, she had enough on her mind and I did not want to burden her any further. Nor did I want to have that discussion at any of our financial meetings. By the time I flipped that house, well maybe it was more like a flop than a flip, it was ten months later and another $20,000 added to our consumer debt. When you start out in $43,000 in consumer debt, you think the only way to go is down, wrong. I, no, we (my wife and I) made a personal financial pledge of $30,000. Why? Please do not ask. However, I truly believe God had something to do with the amount. I hope that if any of you are in debt you avoid making pledges because scripture appears to be against it.

There we were, in Texas lingo, staring down the barrel of a 12 gauge, triple-ought shot gun, ready to blow us to kingdom come (wherever kingdom come is). In the English vernacular, we were pitifully looking at a mountian of debt that was threatening to pull our family apart. Two other scriptures that inspired us to get busy on our debt were; Psalms 62:5 (NKJV) says, *"My soul, wait silently for God alone, for my expectation is from Him."* And Proverbs 21:31 (NKJV) says, *"The horse is prepared for the day of battle, but deliverance is of the Lord."* or The Living Bible says it this way *"Go ahead and prepare for the conflict, but victory comes from God."* So, we had an expectation to become debt free and we got a plan. Then we had to prepare or work the plan, and in the end, trust God for the outcome. Like Chris Hogan of Ramsey Solutions says, "A plan without works is just a wish."

We had looked at our flocks and herds and knew well the condition of our finances. We now had a plan and an expectation. We had completed one of Dave's steps and had $1,000 in our emergency fund. Our next action was Dave's second step, to pay off debt. We listed our debts and decided to pay off the debt that would give us control of the most money in our budget when we paid that item off. Let me explain. Many financial gurus suggest the debt snowball method of paying off your debt. This debt snowball payment accelerates your debt payoff by implementing the "rollover" method. Dave suggests you list your debts from the smallest to the largest and start paying off the smallest debts first. As soon as the first debt is paid off, you use the freed-up monthly payment amount added to payment owed to pay down the next larger debt. The two combined payments accelerated the payoff of the debt. The process continues (rolling like a snowball) until all debts are paid off. When looking at our list of debts, we have several items less than $5,000 and we had several debt items more than $10,000. We decided to go to the middle of the debt list and pay off our $9,000 car note. The payment was $290 a month, no flexibility on that bill. However, the other debt items had flexibility to their payments. We felt that the $290 gave us the most efficiency in paying off items in the debt snowball. We paid the $3,000 we had in our little savings on the car note. Then we squeezed out about $1,000 over the next six months and bu-yah! Our vision on that Vue came to victory, paid-off.

Six months into this plan to be financial free and paying off my wife's car was an exhilarating event. We were pumped with our progress. Well my wife was more excited than I. You see my wife worked at home and I worked outside the home. My wife does not like to use credit cards and refuses to carry one. She asked me to only use cash. Hey that's great when all you have is cash. But when you don't have cash, what else are you supposed to use, except credit cards? We both received the same amount of commission money. My money didn't go as far as hers. If I bought two lunches during our two weeks between pay periods, I was broke. I was forced to carry leftovers for lunch, almost every day. Except when we had fish, didn't want to put that in the office microwave. On occasion I would splurge at the burger place on the dollar menu. A tiny hamburger and tiny fries for $2.14, with water of course. Despite the minor setbacks, it was encouraging to pay off the car. Of course, I continued to drive our 1991 Volvo station wagon. It has become my Dave car. Sorry about that Dave.

Now we had about $1,290 a month to apply to our monthly bills. We had a $3,000 orthodontics bill and a $5,000 credit card bill. After about another six months, we cleaned up those two bills. After a year of working our plan, we had paid off about $17,000 of debt and about $3,000 in interest. Not bad, but we started to slow down and I lost some of the focus needed to fuel the plan. I had pushed my wife to buy a house and flip it. She was very resistant, but I had assured her that the profits from the flip would easily eradicate our remaining debt. Besides, my college age son was with me on the venture and this would be a father-son bonding event. We bought the house and I was putting in most of the work to rehab it. Some of the money we were using to pay bills then had to go pay for the rehab. After 10 months of purchasing that house, we sold it. We received a check for $28,500 from the sale of the house and put another $1,500 with it and paid off the $30,000 pledge we had made. After almost two years into our total money make over, we had paid about $47,000. Now let me say this, Dave Ramsey would not have suggested we purchase and flip a house, especially funded by credit.

Now despite some of the unwise decisions I made, I believe that God was honoring our efforts. Like the two years I received $2,000 bonuses for doing good work at my job. Like the time my wife needed $754 to repair her car and I needed $500 to repair my Dave car(1991 Volvo). I was driving the car illegally because it had not passed an inspection in three years. I prayed "Lord we need money to fix these cars." Several weeks later on a Saturday morning, my son and I arose early to go to Men's Fellowship. As we walked out to the car, I noticed that the car was sitting on top on the curb. Strange I thought, I didn't remember parking it there. My son said Dad I don't think we're driving this car to Fellowship, it's been wrecked. During the night, someone had crushed my Dave car. The person who hit my car left her insurance information on my windshield. Subsequently, the insurance company totaled the vehicle at $1,988, but allowed me to keep the vehicle and sent me a check for about $1,800. We beat the dent out of the car, cashed the check and paid for both cars to be repaired. That was about eleven years ago, and I am still driving that vehicle. Now, that Dave car rolls on until I can get a better Dave car. God answers prayers.

After two and a half years of our war on debt, we had a $14,000 line of credit (partially from the rehab of the flipped house) and a $17,000 Mastercard to pay off. My co-worker told me that her church was teaching Dave Ramsey's Financial Peace University classes that fall on Monday nights. Sorry, I was busy with something called Monday Night Football on ABC. My co-worker and my wife were like two peas in a pod. They were part of the sisterhood and could communicate with each other via mental telepathy or something. I had to tell my wife about the class. Of course, she insisted that we go and dismissed my suggestions to go the following year. Ultimately, the class turned out to be very beneficial, plus Dave was kind of funny. The class reenergized us and gave us even more attentiveness. Our plan was more organized and clearer than ever. With Dave's Seven Baby Steps, we better understood where we were in baby step two, "debt snowball." We began to embrace Dave's "gazelle intensity," making every effort to pay off debt as quickly and effectively as we could. Penny pinching, the practice of being very frugal in giving or spending money or the reluctance to spend money unnecessarily, lived in our house, kind of like a fourth child. Kind of like Charles Dickens' A Christmas Carol' classic tale about a miserable taskmaster named Ebenezer Scrooge, who had visits from a series of ghosts, each showing him his penny-pinching ways by taking him to see his past, present and future. But it was to me a dream, Dave Ramsey's 'A Debt Carol,' where the jokes of Dave Ramsey visited me in my sleep showing me his penny-pinching ways by taking me to see my past, present and future finances. My financial past was dismal, the present was hard work (gazelle intensity) and my future was debt free, living like no other. You are either captive by past decisions or freed by them.

A "BuzzFeed Life" article," 46 Penny-Pinching Ways To Save A Lot Of Money This Year," claimed that little things really do add up. Here are some of the things they suggested:

If you shop at Target, here are some tips: Every Target shopper needs to know this: If the price ends in 8, it will be marked down again. If it ends in a 4, it's the lowest it will be. Target's mark down schedule. - Monday: Kids Clothing, Stationery (office supplies, gift wrap), Electronics. Tuesday: Women's Clothing and Domestics. Wednesday: Men's

Clothing, Toys, Health and Beauty. Thursday: Lingerie, Shoes, Housewares. Friday: cosmetics. Another Target tip: get Target coupons online and stack them with manufacturers coupons.

Make your own liquid hand wash from a bar of soap (I did this as a teenager until my mother caught me and made me quit). For foaming hand wash, re-fill the foaming dispenser with a mixture of one- part dish soap (or body wash) and three parts water (No wonder mine never worked, I didn't use the correct mixture). Learn how to make yogurt in a crock pot (Don't think I'll try this one).

Make your own laundry detergent. A box of regular Tide costs $28 for 68 loads these days. Using this recipe, you can squeeze 96 loads out of $2.88. Save electricity by using the rapid wash setting on your washing machine. You'll notice a difference in your electricity bill. Never buy dryer sheets again. Place a ball of aluminum foil in the dryer with your wet clothes. You can reuse it many, many times and it will remove static cling. Sign up for the Victoria's Secret mailing list. Sure, you'll get an annoying catalog every week, but you'll also get a coupon for a free panty every month. Never buy underwear again! (I like this one, not for me of course). The most effective fly repellent only costs a penny. Place a penny in a zip-loc bag filled with water. For some odd reason, it works. I tried this but, the flies ignored the bags. Maybe it didn't work for me because I did not have the dreaded penny in the bag. I wonder if a Lincoln five-dollar bill would do any better? Now of course Target probably read that article and has changed all their secret codes. I am not totally making fun of these tactics, because they can save you money (like anything else) if you apply them to your life. For us, we mainly said no to these tactics and use fiscal discipline.

Fiscal discipline is sometime difficult. It is hard to say no to kids when you believe your "NO" will jeopardize your child's professional sports career in the NBA, NFL, MLB, US

Figure Skating, PGA, etc., or not to go to lunch with work associates or church members after the last service. What about those $25 birthday parties for your children's friend. You know if your child doesn't go, the other parents are going to talk about you. We paid the minimum on our credit cards while we targeted paying off another bill. We called our financial institutions and talked to them about lowering our interest rates. We refinanced our house mortgage when we could drop down by several interest points. On one occasion, we transferred the balance from one credit card to another. We had our daughter pay part of the cost of her braces. We didn't even have money to initially cover baby step 2 - debt repayment. My wife taught people to read and I worked as a basketball official to earn extra money for the debt. Of course, the way my wife approached me about earning extra money was text book. She asked me what I enjoyed doing. I said playing basketball. She asked me if I could get paid for playing. I answered her, "not like the NBA was going to pay me." She asked me, "could you do something else basketball related and get paid for it, like be a referee?" I said "referee, umm." I had visions of refereeing in the NBA, teeing up some of those rich ball players for arguing with me. Making that call on LeBron James for flopping, because he gets away with all the time. Of course, I said, "yeah, I can do that." And I did for two seasons. I learned a lot about my ancestral heritage doing those two seasons. Fans talked about how I was a "son of a bit-- or blind as a bat."

 Once again, God's sovereign nature is amazing. We had a very bad hail storm which caused a great deal of roof damage to houses in our area. The insurance company estimated our roof replacement at $16,500 and sent us a check for about $13,500 (minus the deduction). At the time, we had been paying off debt like there was no tomorrow. We were down to our last and largest credit card. It was $17,000 and we were paying about $1,500 a month on it. Then the financial company raised the interest on the card. My wife called and questioned their ability to change the interest rate with no notification and no apparent reason. The customer service representative calmly instructed my wife to get our statement, turn it over to the backside and read the fine print. It literally stated that the financial institution could change the rate at any time without notification. My wife thanked the representative and then turned into the real 'Sista Banks.' She looked at me with such invigoration and said, "that's it, we're paying these lenders off, so we won't be slaves anymore." Then she asked, "where is it?" I thought maybe she wanted my gun, maybe we were going down to the local convenient store to get a nonrepayable convenient loan. I didn't know. "Where is that $13,500 check for the roof," she asked me. We took that check and added all the savings we had and paid off the $17,000 credit card bill. Technically, we were debt free - FREEDOM!!! But we still had a roof to replace, so we took the $1,500 that we were paying on the credit card and placed it into our sinking fund account. A sinking fund is an account into which you put money on a regular basis to pay some bill, debt or other expense that will come due in the future. You know you have a life insurance policy which you pay annually, take the annual amount and divide it by 12 and every month place that amount into your sinking fund. Additionally, in our sinking fund, we have other expenses such as: auto insurance, medical and dental visits, furniture items, home and auto repair and sometimes, budget adjusting monies. About a year later (2010), we took the $16,500 out of the sinking fund and had our roof replaced.

    Being debt free except for our mortgage was a great relief. Money fights, uhh...discussions, were reduced to a minimum. My commissions have increased from $10 a week to $20 a week. I felt like Donald Trump, rolling in doe. It might be hard to picture your weekly commission at $10, like it was for me. That's barely one decent lunch a week. Subsequently, as I became wiser in this process, I learned not to focus on what I couldn't buy, but on what I could buy, and sometimes, even on how much I could save. It was a hard but rewarding journey. My efforts were to endure to the end and eventually, there would be a glorious day coming.

There are many debt settlement companies assisting people in this debt-ridden society. Some are helpful, and some are harmful. There are anywhere from five to five thousand steps to help people eliminate debt in this society. Some are helpful, and some are harmful. Listen, whatever company, plan or steps you choose, remember that none of them are etched in stone concerning your financial situation. Some are better for your situation and may not need any changing. Other plans are good but might need some tweaking to work in your specific situation. Wisdom on your part might cause some adjustments to the plan or steps, which you are using. If you have no wisdom, then ask God. Let, thus says The Lord, lead you and your finances. As previously stated, we used Dave Ramsey Seven Baby Steps from his FPU course. The steps were not etched in stone for us, but they were the foundation for us to become debt free

In summary, the process that worked for us went like this: Know well the State of - Not only did we look at our finances, we became attentive, we did something to our finances. We opened additional saving accounts for our different funds; sinking fund, gift fund, car fund, emergency fund and a vacation fund. We had all types of funds except a fun fund. That one came later.

Agreed on the Right Plan - My plan was too loose, my wife's plan was to rigid, Dave's plan was just what we needed at that time (A third independent party). A spending plan we both agreed upon and one that told our finances where to go.

Established an Emergency Fund - We pulled money from several accounts of ours and boo-yah!, we had our $1,000. For many of you, if you consolidate some loose funds, put aside some personal pleasures, skip a few meals out with friends and sell a few items, you also will have $1,000.

Debt - We stopped borrowing money and using my credit card. My wife of course never used credit cards (she's godly). We cut up our credit cards. Some of you might faint, but with a little water in your face, you'll regain consciousness. Then we started eliminating our debt, using the debt snowball method. We listed our debts from the smallest to the largest. We paid off our car first, then paid off the smallest to the largest.

Enhanced Emergency Fund - After being set free from bondage, we started saving for our 3 to 6 months emergency fund, which was $18K to $36K. Two years after becoming debt free, we hit $40,000 in our emergency fund.

Investment/Retirement - We added funds to an old mutual fund we had. We both started Roth IRAs. We started ours at $20 a month and slowly increased them. The pension from my job now covers all our living expenses plus a savings.

Paid Off House - After selling our sixth home and receiving several checks from the Government at my retirement, we had enough liquid savings to pay $160,000 cash for our 3100 sqft. foreclosed and refurbished house.

Build Wealth - The elimination of debt is the building of wealth. You will be surprised how easy it is to build wealth when there is no one else's name on God's money/your finances. When there are no credit card payments, no car payments, no house payments. Just think, how much you could be saving.

Giving - We have now been able to help family members by giving (not loaning) to them in financial difficulties. To help our children, at the time of the births of our grandchildren, buying cars (used of course), and take trips. And we were able to help our church, not just with tithes and offerings, but also by purchasing memberships for the financial class we coordinate.

My wife and I are common folks like you. Like she says, "two black kids from the eastside of Columbus, Ohio, if we can do this, anyone can do this." We just used the common sense that God gave us. In the book of Proverbs, we find many verses on the use of God's money in our pockets. Dave Ramsey swears that if you read the book of Proverbs, you get a degree in economics. Here are some of the verses we have used in our plan to get debt free:

YOU GOT TO KNOW
Proverbs 27:23-24, New King James Version (NKJV) 23 *Be diligent to know the state of your flocks and attend to your herds;24 For riches are not forever, Nor does a crown endure to all generations.*

BE DILIGENT ABOUT YOUR PLAN
Proverbs 12:27 Revised Standard Version (RSV)27 *A slothful man will not catch his prey, but the diligent man will get precious wealth.*

KNOW THE PLAYERS
Proverbs 22:7 (RSV), *The rich rules over the poor, and the borrower is the slave of the lender.*

STOP GOING INTO FURTHER DEBT
Proverbs 11:15 (RSV), *He who gives surety for a stranger will smart for it, but he who hates suretyship is secure.*

LEARN TO SAVE
Proverbs 6:6-8 (NKJV) *Go to the ant, you sluggard! Consider her ways and be wise, Which, having no captain, overseer or ruler, provides her supplies in the summer, and gathers her food in the harvest.*

WEALTH BUILDING BY SMALL INCREASES
Proverbs 13:11 (RSV) 11 *Wealth hastily gotten[a] will dwindle, but he who gathers little by little will increase it.*

BE PATIENT, KEEP THE HOPE
Proverbs 13:12 (RSV) *12 Hope deferred makes the heart sick, but a desire fulfilled is a tree of life.*

TAKE CARE OF FAMILY
Proverbs 13:22 (NKJV) 22 *A good man leaves an inheritance to his children's children, but the wealth of the sinner is stored up for the righteous.*

GIVE
Proverbs 11:24-25 (NKJV) *There is one who scatters yet, increases more; And there is one who withholds more than is right, but it leads to poverty. The generous soul will be made rich, and he who waters will also be watered himself.*

There were several things we did not do because of our finances. One of them was a savings for college for our children. By the time we got to the college savings, all our children were already in college. By the way, for the most part, they were home schooled. We had to send them to college on the Banks Five-Thirty-Third plan. The plan stated if a Banks kid went to college, the Banks family would pay one-third of the cost, the Banks child was required to work the summer and save up one-third (I know, how horrible for us to make our children take ownership in the success of their life) and they could work during college or borrow the remaining one-third. According to Rachael (Ramsey) Cruz, 'Smart Money, Smart Kids,' students who work during college make better grades and learn better time management than those who don't work.

Stephen Curry, Guard, Golden State Warriors, averaging per game; points 29.7, rebounds 5.3 and assists 6.6. He was selected by Golden State in the first round of the 2009 NBA Draft (7th overall). He set an NBA single-season record with 272 three-pointers in the 2012-13 season. Curry finished runner-up for 2009-10 NBA Rookie of the Year Award and was unanimous First Team All-Rookie selection. The thing Curry did was to implement a plan to not only get better, but to become the best scorer in the NBA. During the off season, while many of his compadres were enjoying the pleasures of life, Curry was in a small basement gym for hours everyday, implementing his plan. Guess what, it worked. He is now considered one of the best shooters in NBA history. NBA defenders lose sleep considering how to stop his quick 3-point release, his amazing ball handling skills and ability to get to the rim.

What am I saying? Glad you asked. Having a plan makes a difference. Implementing the plan makes it work. This is 20% head knowledge (plan) and 80% behavior (doing). Do you think plans are important?

This is what the bible has to say about plans:

Proverbs 20:18 (NKJV) *Plans are established by counsel; By wise counsel wage war.*

Proverbs 21:5 (NKJV) *The plans of the diligent lead surely to plenty, but those of everyone who is hasty, surely to poverty*

Proverbs 16:3 (RSV) *Commit your work to the Lord, and your plans will be established.*

What to do? Get a plan. If you are married, get with your spouse, and get a plan. If you are single, get an accountability partner, and get a plan. After you get a plan, then live on it.

According to reference.com, a Belgian draft horse, can pull the equivalent dead weight of approximately 300 to 400 pounds. Two Belgian horses untrained together can pull several thousand pounds. Two Belgian horses trained together have pulled 17,000 dead weight pounds. This is the power of two, working and trained together, increasing their effectiveness.

If you are not doing something with your money, it does not matter how much you have.

REFLECTIONS

Do you have a financial plan?

Is it written?

Do you live on it faithfully?

STEWARDSHIP

Stewards not only know what they have, they also grow what they have.

Givers concentrate on others, the stingy concentrate on themselves and those who want to give, but have not, need to concentrate on being better stewards.

Stewardship is an ethic that embodies the responsible planning and management of resources. The concepts of stewardship can be applied to the environment and nature, economics, health, property, information, theology, etc. Stewardship originally consisted of the tasks of a domestic steward, from stig (house, hall) and weard (ward, guard, guardian, keeper). In the beginning, stewardship related to the duties of the household servant for bringing food and drink to the castle's dining hall. Stewardship responsibilities were then expanded to include most everything the domestic needs of the entire household. Commercially, stewardship attends to the domestic service of passengers on trains, ships, airplanes or customers in restaurants. Today, stewardship is generally recognized as the manager, shepherd or safeguard the property of others. Simply put, stewardship is the management of someone else's property.

Now let's get Churchy. Psalm 24:1(KJV) *"The earth is the Lord's, and all its fullness, the world and those who* dwell therein." The Bible says God created the world and the universe, therefore all is his. When you make something out of nothing, you can say, I made it, it's mine. That is what God did and He's got the t-shirt to prove it. That is Bible 101. But there are some of us who haven't gotten the words "all its fullness." Since we are talking about money, let me repeat this scripture; Haggai 2:8 (NKJV) *"The silver is Mine, and the gold is Mine,"* says the Lord of hosts. The Voice translates this way, *"You see, all the silver and all the gold in this world already belong to Me."* The hood; "It's God's money yo!" So, it's not just all about the Benjamins, it's also all about the stuff. Look, if it's not my money, then surely, it's not my stuff, that I bought with the money, that wasn't mine. I began to look at all the stuff we had. Holy smoke, where did all this stuff come from. When the government contracted movers came to relocate us from Texas to Washington DC, they even asked, does all this stuff go? Well a quarter of our stuff (one truck) went to DC, another quarter went to Good Will, friends and the trash and the final two-quarters (two and one-half trucks) went into storage.

I recall Dave Ramsey saying, "sell so much stuff that the kids think they are next." Well I am not much of a salesman, but we had a garage sale. Now neither me nor my wife wanted to do the garage sale, especially me because I would miss our church Men's Basketball Fellowship. Therefore, we ended up giving most of the stuff away. I remember we had a dog cage in the garage sale that we had purchased for $60. We were asking $20 for the cage. Several people had looked at it and did not really need one (at that price). This one man said, "well will you take $10 for the cage." I really wasn't in a negotiating mood and told the man no. After the man left, I decided to terminate my participation in that garage. I took a piece of paper and wrote this word on it, "FREE." The next man who stopped, saw the "FREE" sign couldn't believe it. He said he was looking for a dog cage and said that the cage was a good one and asked me if I was sure it was free. I said yeah, it's free. He said let me pay you something for it and I told him no. Others came by, took advantage of the FREE stuff and left happy. The people were happy, I could now go to the Men's Fellowship (because most of the stuff was gone) so I was happy, all God's children were happy, until my wife returned and saw that FREE sign. She wasn't happy. She pointed out the error of my ways, in no uncertain terms. Was I a good steward of what God had entrusted me? Could I have done better with what God had entrusted me? I know you are saying come on, it was a dog cage. Are you telling me that deal affects the Kingdom of God?

Hugh Whelchel is Executive Director of the Institute for Faith, Work & Economics and author of "How Then Should We Work?": In a blog on stewardship the question was asked, "What does stewardship look like in our lives today?" In an article by Whelchel on November 26, 2012, he mentioned that many Christians today only associate the idea of stewardship with sermons they have heard regarding church budgets and building programs. In the article, Whelchel quoted C. S. Lewis in Mere Christianity: "Every faculty you have, your power of thinking or of moving your limbs from moment to moment is given you by God. If you devoted every moment of your whole life exclusively to His service, you could not give Him anything that was not in a sense His own already." Whelchel and the Institute for Faith, Work & Economics, also sees the idea of biblical stewardship as something much more expansive than a church's building program. They believe it is where the concepts of faith, work, and economics intersect. Whelchel also quoted from an essay entitled Leadership is Stewardship written by Bill Peel, of The High Calling. Peel suggests that there are four important principles about biblical stewardship we must understand:

1. The principle of ownership. Psalms 24:1(NKJV) *The earth is the Lord's, and all its fullness, the world and those who dwell therein.* God owns everything, we are simply managers or administrators acting on his behalf. Therefore, stewardship expresses our obedience regarding the administration of everything God has placed under our control, which is all encompassing.
2. The principle of responsibility. In explaining responsibility, Peel writes, "Although God gives us all things richly to enjoy, nothing is ours. Nothing really belongs to us. God owns everything; Owners have rights; stewards have responsibilities." And we are responsible to manage his holdings according to his desires and purposes.
3. The principle of accountability. A steward is one who manages the possessions of another. Like the servants in the Parable of the Talents, we will be called to give an account of how we have administered everything we have been given, including our time, money, abilities, information, wisdom, relationships, and authority.
4. The principle of reward. Paul writes: Colossians 3:23-24 (NKJV) *"And whatever you do, do it heartily, as to the Lord and not to men, knowing that from the Lord you will receive the reward of the inheritance; for you serve the Lord Christ."* The Bible shows us in the parables of the Kingdom that faithful stewards who do the master's will with the master's resources can expect to be rewarded incompletely in this life, but fully in the next.

However, when I see these principles, I can't help but think about the verse from Proverbs 27:23(NKJV), *"Be diligent to know the state of your flocks, and attend to your herds;"* It is important to be responsible (this world needs more of that) and we need to be held accountable (for all our actions), but we also need to know what we are being responsible to and being held accountable for.

The Banks Family owns twenty acres of land in East Texas. Land inherited from my grandfather. For years, my siblings and I were only concerned with three acres which had been sectioned off by my grandfather for my father and mother in the 1950's. However, recently an oil company contacted the family, interested in drilling for oil in the area. All I could think about was the song from the Beverly Hillbillies. "Come listen to a story about a man named Ted, A poor government worker but he kept his family fed. Then one day in a bad working mood, An oil company called about drilling for crude. Oil that is, Black gold, Texas-T." Hey, don't try to steal my song. Listen, once the oil company completed a search of the persons who had an "interest"(persons who have a right to claim some ownership in the property) in the property, I found out that my siblings and I have interest in the entire twenty acres. Royalty checks are determined upon the percentage of acreage in which you had an interest. Ching-ching. The more acres, the larger the checks. Even though we had an interest, we did not know it. You see knowing what you have can sometimes make all the difference in the world. It is difficult for the steward to effectively take care of the Masters property when the steward doesn't know with what the Master has entrusted him. Know well the condition of your flocks.

My Big Momma, that's Grandmother in Texan, was a loving, kind and wise person. I can't seem to recall her ever standing erect. She walked with a slight stoop in her back, I guess from years of hard work. I always loved sitting with my Big Momma. She would tell me about God and give me words of wisdom. However, not all of those words of wisdom were out of the Bible. She used to say to me, "You can find a boogie bear behind every bush, if that's what you're looking for." First of all, I was never-ever looking for a boogie bear, which I thought lived under my bed and ate little children. Secondly, as I got older, I understood my Big Momma to say, whatever in life you are looking for you will find it, wherever you look. When I was a young boy, I looked for racism, I found it behind every bush, in every white person. As a teenager, without a father, I was angry and looked for anger and found it behind every bush, in every situation in my life. But as I became older and found the Lord, I then looked for wisdom and I found it behind the tree of life. I looked for grace and found it behind every Word of God.

Subsequently, when I look for stewardship, I find it in it in virtually every scripture. To me, the very first verse in the Bible speaks about stewardship, *"In the beginning God created the heavens and the earth,"* (Genesis 1:1(KJV)). When you are the creator, you have total ownership over all things, and to miss this starting point is like building a house without a builder's square and a level. You might get it built, but you won't have square rooms and when you roll out of bed, you will roll because your floors will not be level. To me, the doctrine of stewardship makes sense when I understand the fact that God is the Creator and all is under his ownership. If all belongs to God, then we obviously are not owners, but stewards. Someone who is managing someone else's property. In Luke 15 (NKJV) verses 3-5 says: *"So He spoke this parable to them, saying: What man of you, having a hundred sheep, if he loses one of them, does not leave the ninety-nine in the wilderness, and go after the one which is lost until he finds it? And when he has found it, he lays it on his shoulders, rejoicing."* and verses 8-10: *"Or what woman, having ten silver coins, if she loses one coin, does not light a lamp, sweep the house, and search carefully until she finds it? And when she has found it, she calls her friends and neighbors together saying, "Rejoice with me, for I have found the piece which I lost!"* We know that one of the things the Lord is talking about is the restoration of repentant sinners. I see that, but I also see stewardship. In the previous parables, both the man and the woman knew what they had in their possession. How did either one know they were missing one? They would have not known had they not been diligent and attentive to the state of their flocks and herds. I have conducted many theft investigations, and one question I always asked the victims was, "do you know when the property was taken or when was the last time you saw it?" If you tell me you saw it that day, we are cooking with gas and have a hot trail to follow in the investigation. If you tell me you last saw it about six months ago, or can't remember the last time you saw it, I packed up my government issued detective kit and my Bazooka decoder ring and I went home. I would have told the victim, "this trail is colder than a Wisconsin winter, call me if you find out who committed this crime." You have to diligently know what you have and at least have seen it. Because the man and woman knew what they had, then they knew what was missing and because they knew what was missing, they knew what to look for. And because they had been attentive, they knew where to look, he in the wilderness and her in her home. Knowing where to look for what you are looking for is half the battle.

Additionally, in Luke 15:11-22 (NKJV), we find the parable of the Prodigal Son. *"Then He said: A certain man had two sons. And the younger of them said to his father, "Father, give me the portion of goods that falls to me." So he divided to them his livelihood. And not many days after, the younger son gathered all together, journeyed to a far country, and there wasted his possessions with prodigal living. But when he had spent all, there arose a severe famine in that land, and he began to be in want. Then he went and joined himself to a citizen of that country, and he sent him into his fields to feed swine. And he would gladly have filled his stomach with the pods that the swine ate, and no one gave him anything. But when he came to himself, he said, How many of my father's hired servants have bread enough and to spare, and I perish with hunger! I will arise and go to my father, and will say to him, Father, I have sinned against heaven and before you, and I am no longer worthy to be called your son. Make me like one of your hired servants. And he arose and came to his father. But when he was still a great way off, his father saw him and had compassion, and ran and fell on his neck and kissed him. And the son said to him, "Father, I have sinned against heaven and in your sight and am no longer worthy to be called your son. But the father said to his servants, bring out the best robe and put it on him, and put a ring on his hand and sandals on his feet."*

Once again, an example of God's restorative desire for the repentant sinner. However, the word prodigal means extravagant wasteful, so named the parable. This parable is not called the restorative son, or the son who took his inheritance and lost it all, or even loser son. It's called the prodigal because the son wasted his inheritance. I think that is kind of related to stewardship. We see the prodigal son's dad who had apparently been a good steward of what God had given him to manage. The father then passed the rightful portion (inheritance) of his property to his younger son. The rest is history. The son squandered his inheritance and returned home to live in his Father's basement. This story should not be a surprise to any of us in the way it ended. Always, there are several schools of thought regarding the father's action to give his young, immature son his rightful inheritance.

One of the thoughts is that no parent should place an amount of wealth or resources in their child's hand when that child has not shown that they are adequately mature to manage such resources. If a son or daughter does not have the maturity, character or experience in stewardship to manage the gift, then that parent has placed their child in a precarious situation to fail. I know as a parent, we not only want the best for our children, we also want to help them greatly (if possible), especially with their financial responsibilities. We pray for our children's financial success, then we sometimes try to microwave their situation by giving them everything they need to be equal to our financial situation, the same situation that took us twenty-five years to achieve. You see, we managed and matured with our finances as it says in the book of Proverbs, by small increases. But, when we or our children try to microwave their life style equal to ours in several years what took many of us many years, the maturing process is often crippled.

Another school of thought, which did not put the blame on the father in this parable. Saying that he did not have to exercised prudent judgement as a steward in his decision to give his son his portion of the inheritance. Understanding that the Old Testament requires the father to bequeath his possessions to his sons (Deuteronomy 21:16 (NKJV)). In the parable however, it did not seem as if it was the right day to bequeath to the son by the father. The young son demanded his share of the father's possessions. How wise was the Father giving a vast part of his possessions to a character flawed, immature child? Was there any consideration of the son's stewardship ability of his newly acquired wealth? The son squandered all and came back home broke. He failed the stewardship test. How many of us have failed the stewardship test? But, the son returned home differently, a better man because of his experience. Somewhere in that pig pen, the boy found more than some pods, he found some humility and repentance. In John Maxwell's book, "It's Just a Thought," he quotes David Jeremiah, "You have to give up, to go up." What is the price for humility? How wise was that Father? The rest of the story is restored relationship.

In Luke 16 (NKJV), Jesus gives the parable of the unjust steward. It says: *"He also said to His disciples: There was a certain rich man who had a steward, and an accusation was brought to him that this man was wasting his goods. So, he called him and said to him, what is this I hear about you? Give an account of your stewardship, for you can no longer be steward. Then the steward said within himself, What shall I do? For my master is taking the stewardship away from me. I cannot dig; I am ashamed to beg. I have resolved what to do, that when I am put out of the stewardship, they may receive me into their houses, so he called every one of his master's debtors to him, and said to the first, how much do you owe my master? And he said, a hundred measures of oil. So he said to him, take your bill, and sit down quickly and write fifty. Then he said to another, and how much do you owe? So, he said, a hundred measures of wheat. And he said to him, take your bill, and write eighty. So the master commended the unjust steward because he had dealt shrewdly. For the sons of this world are more, shrewd in their generation than the sons of light."*

I didn't have to look hard for this boogie bear. This parable is clearly about stewardship - management of finances and responsibilities. The steward is an employee of a rich landlord, managing the landlord's assets. One day the steward was called in by the landlord due to an accusation that he (steward) had been wasting the landlord's assets. Note that the difference between the prodigal and the unjust steward is that the steward had been only wasting his Lord's resources while the prodigal was guilty of "extravagant wasteful" of his own resources. Therefore, the landlord called the steward in to give an account of his assets. I heard a preacher say, "People only do what you inspect." If the landlord failed to check on his steward, then the steward probably started to think that he was the owner. It's dangerous when we think our decisions have no repercussions or consequences. When I was an agent for the Federal Government, every 30 days, we had the dreaded case review with our supervisor. I would gather up my investigative files, take them to my supervisor's desk and review the actions on each investigation for the past month. If I had done something productive on all 25 cases then I was patted on the back, but if not, I was given corrective actions to conduct on the investigations which were lacking. Even though they were my investigations, I did not own them. At any time, my supervisor could have reassigned any of my investigations to another agent. You see, even though they were my investigations, the cases and all the resources used in the investigation belonged to the Government. I worked investigations for the betterment of society, to punish the bad guy. Ultimately, it was always the Government that determined the fate of the investigation. The resources belonged to the rich landlord who had the power of reassigning his resources to another steward for the betterment of his finances.

The unjust steward was caught between his boss who said, you're fired and the customers with whom he had been doing business. The steward had a simple plan, since he could not go to the boss, he decided to go to the customers and said, "I'll do you a favor if you do me a favor. I will reduce what you owe my boss, just don't forget me later." Bottom line was that the landlord gave props to the unjust steward. It is not my word, the Bible says it. Let's look at some other translations: *And his lord commended the unrighteous steward because he had done wisely: for the sons of this world are for their own generation wiser than the sons of the light,* (Luke 16:8 American Standard Version (ASV)). *And [his] master praised the dishonest (unjust) manager for acting shrewdly and prudently; for the sons of this age are shrewder and more prudent and wiser in [relation to] their own generation [to their own age and kind] than are the sons of light,* (Luke 16:8, Amplified Bible, Classic Edition (AMPC)). *The master praised his dishonest manager for looking out for himself so well. That's how it is! The people of this world look out for themselves better than the people who belong to the light.; Now here's a surprise: The master praised the crooked manager! And why? Because he knew how to look after himself. Streetwise people are smarter in this regard than law-abiding citizens. They are on constant alert, looking for angles, surviving by their wits. I want you to be smart in the same way, but for what is right using every adversity to stimulate you to creative survival, to concentrate your attention on the bare essentials, so you'll live, really live, and not complacently just get by on good behavior,* (Luke 16:8, The Message (MSG)).

Look at some of the various translations of that parable and the diversity or words that were used to describe the actions of the fired steward; He acted wisely and wiser than the children of light (us if we are confessing Christ as our Lord and Savoir); He acted shrewdly and prudent and more prudent and wiser than the children of light; cleverly and more-clever; That he was looking out for himself and that the world looked out for themselves better than the children of light look out for themselves; He acted prudently and was more prudent; He had done a smart thing and was smarter; He acted astutely and was more-astute; Smart and smarter; and acted with shrewdness and was more-shrewd. If the steward being unjust was commended for his unjust ways, how much more should we, God's just people, be commended for our just and proper ways of handling God's resources? But the master commended this steward for being shrewd. Now, I ain't no walking dictionary, but I always thought that the word shrewd was a demeaning term. I know it's hard to believe, but I was wrong. Shrewd means to be astute, keen, to act with foresight. When the master commended the crooked steward for being shrewd, he was saying, "hey dude, that's pretty sharp of you to come up with that scheme, but you are still fired."

When I was a young man, I applied for a position with the Federal Bureau of Investigation (FBI) and the Naval

Investigative Service (NIS), later becoming the Naval Criminal Investigative Service (NCIS). The employment process for each of the agencies was long and detailed. I had to explain to the FBI and the NIS a situation that occurred while I was attending college at Kent State University. I had unintentionally omitted a post office box I had used while attending college. The post office box was attached to an apartment that I had for one year while going to school. Because no one in my family had a credit card (except for me) that I needed in order to get the apartment, therefore I took on an alias name and applied for the apartment. Then I co-signed for the apartment, using my real name and my credit card to close out the deal. The FBI accused me of creating a fraudulent identity, of utilizing someone else's social security number, of not being truthful. I was polygraphed and eventually, my application process was terminated. At one point in time, I thought the hiring agent was going to open an investigation and arrest me. However, when I told this occurrence to the hiring agent at the NIS, he commended me for being sharp (shrewd) and witty. And said I was the kind of creative thinker they were looking for, Buyah! I became a Special Agent for the NIS, and I didn't go to jail. Alleluia!

When you consider the bottom line, every biblical doctrine pertains to man's relationship to God. Stewardship also defines a man's relationship to God. It says that God is the owner and man is the manager. When our children were teen-aggravators, they would say, "why do we have to clean our rooms, they are just the way we like them and besides, they are not hurting anyone." We would respond, second of all your room can hurt you because there is some green fungus growing on those plates on your desks. My wife started charging them money every time she found kitchen items in their rooms. First of all, we told them they do err. The rooms were not theirs, but ours. We checked the house title and their names were not on it. Then we told them, because we paid the mortgage and the bills, we were the owners. In life, I have found out that owners make up the rules. One time, we made a request to one of our children, to which they failed to conduct. To help our child to understand our request, as owners, we removed our door from the room in which they were sleeping. And when that child asked about their door, we simply reminded them of the first rule, the door, like the room, was not theirs, but ours. They did what we asked and we replaced our door to the room they were sleeping in.

God is a lot wiser than me. I know, what a shocker. That's alright, I can live with that because He's also wiser than you. Instead of threatening to blow our doors off, so that we would proper manage what He has given us, God makes us co-workers in His service. Paul writes in, 1 Corinthians 3:9 (NKJV) *"For we are God's fellow workers; you are God's field, you are God's building."* Stewardship directs our purpose in life and explains what we are to do in this world with the property and resources assigned to us by God. Stewardship (of property) is God giving His property to His people and His people managing those properties according to God's Word.

Like I said, when I began to look into the Word of God regarding stewardship, I began to see stewardship behind virtually every Word of God. In addition to the above mentioned principles, four stages of stewardship came to me, and when my Pastor, Rex Johnson, preached a message on giving, I perceived a fifth stage.

The stages are as follows:

1. KNOW - A steward must be diligent to know what of possessions they are in control. We cannot manage effectively if we don't know what we have. A great coach said, "You must know what you have, before you can make a game plan." Well actually, I said that, but I did coach my son's 10-year old basketball team. Maybe some coach will agree to that statement. Besides, how

do you know to use something, if you don't know you have it?
2. WHOSE - A steward must know whose stuff they are managing. Either you are going to be a manager of God's stuff or you are going to be a servant of your stuff.
3. FAITHFUL - A steward must be trustworthy or loyal to his or her position. Woody Allen said, "Eighty percent of success is showing up." I think most accomplishments comes from daring to begin and the faithfulness to endure to the end.
4. DO - A steward must do something with the stuff they are managing. Theodore Roosevelt said, "Do what you can with what you have, where you are." His grandson, Franklin D. Roosevelt said, "Above all, try something." The steward's job is not only to know what the Master has given him, to utilize what he has been given, but also to increase what the Master has given him.
5. GRATITUDE - A steward is grateful for what he can do for his Master. Always show gratitude. What you take for granted will eventually be taken away. In the end, the thing you missed the most, is what you had the least gratitude for. Remember, the things you take for granted, someone else is praying to get.

I hear the theologians out there screaming at me saying that stewardship is more than the management of God's property. They are asking, what about the management of God's other resources? Calm down, don't lose your salvation, I get it. Colossians 1:24-26 (NKJV) *"I now rejoice in my sufferings for you, and fill up in my flesh what is lacking in the afflictions of Christ, for the sake of His body, which is the church, of which I became a minister according to the stewardship from God which was given to me for you, to fulfill the word of God, the mystery which has been hidden from ages and from generations, but now has been revealed to His saints."*

1 Corinthians 9:16-18(NKJV) *"For if I preach the gospel, I have nothing to boast of, for necessity is laid upon me; yes, woe is me if I do not preach the gospel! For if I do this willingly, I have a reward; but if against my will, I have been entrusted with a stewardship. What is my reward then? That when I preach the gospel, I may present the gospel of Christ without charge, that I may not abuse my authority in the gospel."*

1 Corinthians 4:1(NKJV) *"Let a man so consider us, as servants of Christ and stewards of the mysteries of God."*

1 Peter 4:9-11(NKJV) *"Be hospitable to one another without grumbling. As each one has received a gift, minister it to one another, as good stewards of the manifold grace of God. If anyone speaks, let him speak as the oracles of God. If anyone ministers, let him do it as with the ability which God supplies, that in all things God may be glorified through Jesus Christ, to whom belong the glory and the dominion forever and ever. Amen."*

In these scriptures, we see the Apostle Paul fulfillment to stewardship from God as the ministering of the Word of God to the body of Christ. That he (Paul) was entrusted with this calling to properly manage God's Word through preaching without abusing his authority. Not only to share the known Word and oracles of God, but also mysteries of God. Finally, Paul said that we are to be good stewards of God's multifaceted grace of the gifts we receive from God. Spiritual and physical gifts.

Therefore, stewardship that is required of us is more

than how we manage property, stuff, finances or even our faithfulness in paying God's tithes and offerings. It is even more than the management of time, relations, environment, health or ourselves. Obedient stewardship says we do not have the right of control over ourselves or our property, that God has that control. Author Bill Peel, he said, "Leadership is stewardship and I see stewardship as success." The more obedient a person is in stewardship, the more successful the person's life. Why? Because obedient stewardship places our focus on properly managing of all God's resources. And it's amazing how our lives are better when we don't live our lives focused on ourselves. Being obedient stewards of Christ motivates us to Christ like deeds concerning God's resources. Where Jesus is our example of obedient stewardship propels us to success. When we handle God's resources correctly, we always operate in the plus, not in the negative. With our finances, we should operate in the black, not overspending or utilizing credit that puts us in the red. We should properly use and not abuse anything God has given us. If we don't properly use it, but abuse it, God can easily find someone who will use it correctly.

We all remember the parable of the talents. Matthew 25:14-19 (NKJV) *"For the kingdom of heaven is like a man traveling to a far country, who called his own servants and delivered his goods to them. And to one he gave five talents, to another two, and to another one, to each according to his own ability; and immediately he went on a journey. Then he who had received the five talents went and traded with them, and made another five talents. And likewise, he who had received two gained two more also. But he who had received one went and dug in the ground and hid his lord's money. After a long time the lord of those servants came and settled accounts with them."* The lord told the two servants who had doubled their talents, *"Well done, good and faithful servant; you were faithful over a few things, I will make you ruler over many things." But to the other servant, the lord said, "You wicked and lazy servant, So, you ought to have deposited my money with the bankers, and at my coming I would have received back my own with interest. Therefore' take the talent from him, and give it to him who has ten talents."* The lord was looking for faithfulness, proper usage and an increase. For those stewards who practiced faithfulness, proper usage and an increase, they were rewarded. The steward who did not practice faithfulness, proper usage and an increase, he was not rewarded. In fact, that servant was de-rewarded, OK, not a word, but he was re-rewarded, now that's a word, kind of. Re-rewarded is not a compensation word, but a word regarding position in an army's attack formation. It is similar to the rear guard of a moving army. Often, it is the positions of the least use persons and those that did little. Those who do least lose their place of much authority to a place with little authority. You may think it's bad to take from the one who has little and give it to the one who has more. But the lord also said, *"For to everyone who has, more will be given, and he will have abundance; but from him who does not have, even what he has will be taken away,"* Matthew 25:29 (NKJV) God gave to these three servants. Why? What was His expectations? I believe that God expected those servants to do something with those talents, He expected getting more in return than what He loaned out. He expects an increase.

Listen, if you had two college age children at home and one car to divide among them. And you told them both they could use the vehicle for work and school, but they had to fairly share the vehicle to meet their respective schedules. At the end of six months, you sat down with them to review their care and usage of the vehicle. Suppose you found out the first child used the car to get to work and school and was often late and had subsequently lost his job. The first child very seldom put gas in the vehicle, never did any needed repairs on the vehicle, received two moving violations and had a minor accident with the vehicle. The second child properly used the vehicle for school and his job, arranged for an oil change and repairs on the vehicle. Was the one who regularly filled the vehicle up with gas and washed it weekly. If you had to give the vehicle to one of your children, which one would it be?

Proverbs 13:4(NKJV) says, *"The soul of a lazy man desires, and has nothing; But the soul of the diligent shall be made rich."*

Friend of mine, God is the owner and we are his stewards. We are required to manage God's assets with which he has trusted us. The problem with ownership mentality is that it breeds entitlement and hoarding. On the other hand, stewardship breeds accountability, responsibility, generosity and gratitude. To be repetitive, stewardship requires that we understand that we are not the owners, but the managers. Dave Ramsey says, "We've got to help them stop thinking like owners and start acting like managers." I hate to borrow my neighbor's stuff because I am so concerned that I will break it and have too buy them another one. In those cases, I might as well buy the item and not be concerned if it breaks or not. In other words, I treat property differently depending on who it belongs too. When I get it into my head that this property belongs to God, my relationship with the property changes. I take better care of it.

The ultimate question, is this: Is Christ the Lord of my life or is it stuff? Am I putting stuff before Christ? Godly stewardship is an expression of our total obedience to our Lord and Savior, Jesus Christ. Stewardship to Christ acknowledges that we do not have the right of control over ourselves or our stuff, God has control. It also means that as godly stewards, we are managers of that which belongs to God, and we are under his authority as we attend to his agenda.

As a steward you must know what you have been entrusted with and formulate a plan with God to develop it, but the question how far do we go. Do we endanger a family's health and well-being when we purchase generic labeled food items instead of the top brand items? Do we shop at used stores to purchase experienced clothing and furniture items? How far do we go? Do we challenge the Internal Revenue Service (IRS) when we think that we have been taxed unfairly and we are not going to give most of it to Cesar anymore? Do we draw the line and say you cannot have any more of the master's money? Moses was faced with a similar situation. He defied the Great Pharaoh by asking him to let my people and livestock go free. The Pharaoh said no. What did Moses do?

Exodus 10:21-26(NKJV) 21 Then the Lord said to Moses, "Stretch out your hand toward heaven, that there may be darkness over the land of Egypt, darkness which may even be felt." 22 So Moses stretched out his hand toward heaven, and there was thick darkness in all the land of Egypt three days. 23 They did not see one another; nor did anyone rise from his place for three days. But all the children of Israel had light in their dwellings.

24 Then Pharaoh called to Moses and said, "Go, serve the Lord; only let your flocks and your herds be kept back. Let your little ones also go with you."

25 But Moses said, "You must also give us sacrifices and burnt offerings, that we may sacrifice to the Lord our God. 26 Our livestock also shall go with us; not a hoof shall be left behind. For we must take some of them to serve the Lord our God, and even we do not know with what we must serve the Lord until we arrive there."

Notice something here, just like the world, Pharaoh demanded Israel's wealth. The world demands our finances through our desires, convenience and greed. When we have to have it and we can't afford it, we charge it. Then the banks demand our finances. When we have to drive it and we can't afford it, then we finance it. Or when the Joneses get it and we have to equal it because we were greedy for it, then we borrow it and the finance companies demand our finances. But Moses said to Pharaoh, no. Saying no to the Pharaoh was normally like a death sentence. See how adamant Moses was about God's stuff. He said not only are we taking our flocks and herds (our wealth), we will not leave one hoof behind. Then, Moses was saying we need our wealth, not only for sacrificing but also to worship God. Now, we need our finances, not only to provide for our families, but also to worship God.

We need to be adamant today about our finances. Look, when my cable bill went up $2.00, you bet I called. I want the telephone, utilities and any other company that sends us a bill, to expect a call from me when that bill goes up. Why? Because it's not my money, but I am responsible for God's money. Also, I don't want to be the victim of the monthly bill creep. Our bill creeps-up (increases) by a few cents every month until it's gone up several dollars. Then I call, the company stops the creep. Maybe they were just trying to see how high they could creep-up before I called and said, "What the creep?"

Why this passage from Exodus? Because after the plague of darkness came the plague of the firstborn came. Where at midnight, all the first-born in the land of Egypt, including their cattle died. There was crying in all Egypt, because there was not a house where at least one person was not dead.

Exodus 12:31-36(NIV) says, *During the night Pharaoh summoned Moses and Aaron and said, "Up! Leave my people,* *you and the Israelites! Go, worship the Lord as you have requested. <u>Take your flocks and herds</u>, <u>as you have said</u>, and go. And also bless me."*

The Egyptians urged the people to hurry and leave the country. "For otherwise," they said, "we will all die!" So, the people took their dough before the yeast was added and carried it on their shoulders in kneading troughs wrapped in clothing. The Israelites did as Moses instructed and asked the Egyptians for articles of silver and gold and for clothing. The Lord had made the Egyptians favorably disposed toward the people, and they gave them what they asked for; so they plundered the Egyptians.

Just a couple of things about these scriptures. Obviously, Pharaoh and the Egyptians had had enough with the plagues. Pharaoh not only released the Israelites, but also their flocks and herds. He released their wealth and made this statement. "as you have said." Pharaoh yielded to Moses stance and gave him what he asked for, their flocks and herds, not one hoof. Moses said it and it came to pass. There is power in the words we use. Declare it and dare it to happen. Kings are subject to our words when our God is behind them. And after seeing the power of God Almighty, he asked that he be blessed also. In their fearfulness, the Egyptians also urged the Israelites to leave. Moses seized the opportunity and had the Israelites to ask to Egyptians for articles of silver and gold and for clothing. Remember what is said in Deuteronomy 8:18(RSV), *"You shall remember the Lord your God, for it is he who gives you power to get wealth.* Therefore, God made the Egyptians show favor to the Israelites and they gave them what they asked for; so, they plundered the Egyptians. The Israelites added to their prosperity. Some translations say the Israelites carried away the wealth of the Egyptians. In Proverbs 13:22(Good News Translation (GBT)) says,

Know Well (Wealth) Your Flocks and Herds

"Good people will have wealth to leave to their grandchildren, but the wealth of sinners will go to the righteous." Because of Moses' adamant refusal to leave one hoof behind, the situation progressed to the final plague. Sometimes things get worse, before they get better. When you take that needed stand for your finances by refusing to use that credit card, to go to the payday loan place, borrow that money from Aunt Ju-Ju, sign those Reverse Mortgage papers, buy that car that you can only afford the monthly payments, or try to keep up with the Joneses. Remember, not one hoof.

Finally, let me finish with this. I can feel some of your thoughts (not really), saying that "Ted is really a cheap person (thanks for the kind words)," but it's not always me. The other day, my wife and I shopped at a grocery store, a great place to shop when you are frugal. After packing the bags and loading all 50 bags (seemed that many) into the car, my wife noticed an error on our bill. We had three cans of tuna fish but was charged for four. That 64 cents for that one can began to stir her. Now not so much me because I had visions on unloading those 100 bags (they seem to grow), taking them back inside the store, taking everything out and showing them that we only had three cans of tuna fish, all for 64 cents. My wife said, "I am going back in." At the same time, I was thinking, I am not going in. I went in with her. She only took the bill. My wife showed the bill to the clerk and the clerk gave her 64 cents. We go to the store about ten times a week. If we were shorted 64 cents every time we went, we would be out about $25 a month. That is $300 a year. Listen, if you invest that $300.00 at 8.000% annually for 40 years, your investment could yield $77,716.96. Now that's a lot of tuna, sorry. One can of tuna, like one hoof can make a difference. Not one hoof. I know this is not a big deal and its only 64 cents, but we must take a stand for God's money and our finances. Not one hoof. Prosperity begins with knowing how many hooves you have. Not one hoof left behind. Wealth is built little by little. Your little flocks and herds have hooves. Not one hoof left behind.

The harder you work for your finances, the harder it should be to give them up.

REFLECTIONS

To you, what is the difference between a steward and an owner?

Are you an owner of your wealth and property?

Think of a time that you stood up for God's money, your finances, against an unrighteous request?

PROSPERITY

"Then you say in your heart, 'My power and the might of my hand have gained me this wealth. "And you shall remember the Lord your God, for it is He who gives you power to get wealth, that He may establish His covenant which He swore to your fathers, as it is this day." Deuteronomy 8:17-18 (NKJV)

In the fall of 1999, my job situation with the NCIS was in dire straits. We had been assigned to the Chicago office for eight years. It was an office that did not have a great reputation for its morale. During my nine years there, the agents suffered through brutal winters, a shortage of personnel, the death of a sibling, the death of several agent's parents (including my mother), the death of an agent, the death of a work associate and a host of other bizarre working conditions. My wife and I were so ready to leave that office. In addition to submitting transfer requests, I also filed applications with several other federal investigative agencies. It was a very emotional time for us. We were frustrated, we cried, we prayed and hoped God would do something. One evening while we were in one of those spiritual battles, I went down stairs to our basement. I was confused and frustrated in my spirit, wondering if even God would work something out on our behalf. When I got to the bottom of the stairs, I was nearly in tears. Then I heard a still small voice that simply said, "Trust Me." I said, "God, you are Top Dog." I hope that was not disrespectful. I stopped trying to do it all and let the Lord do whatever. Shortly thereafter, things changed, not in my physical world, but in my spiritual world. We obeyed and had faith in God that he would take care of us because he said, "Trust Me." God blessed us and gave us prosperity. Twelve years later, five houses ($826K in mortgages), another job, four moves, $86K in consumer debt and we paid cash for the house we now live in. For real, that is God's blessing. And God does not bless something unless he is involved in it. Whatever God is involved in, he increases it. And whatever he increases, he prospers. That's prosperity.

The definition of prosperity is a successful, flourishing, or thriving condition, especially in financial respects; good fortune; prosperous circumstances, characterized by financial success or completeness. It is like a journey through life, going from an unsuccessful situation to a successful, prosperous, thriving, abundant life circumstances. Like what our family went through, debt to no debt, mortgage to no mortgage, broke to blessed. Prosperity or the root word "prosper" appears over 60 to 80 times in the Old and New Testaments (depending upon the translation). When we look at many of those scriptures, we see a lot of prospering going on for God's people. Whether it was Abraham, Isaac, Jacob, Esau, Joseph, Job, etc., these were all men who obeyed the Lord. In fact, prosperity is a blessing from God when people obey. Joshua 1:8 (NKJV) says, *"This Book of the Law shall not depart from your mouth, but you shall meditate in it day and night, that you may observe to do according to all that is written in it. For then you will make your way prosperous, and then you will have good success."* Psalm 1:1-3(KJV) says, *"Blessed is the man who walks not in the counsel of the ungodly, nor stands in the path of sinners, nor sits in the seat of the scornful; But his delight is in the law of the Lord, and in His law, he meditates day and night. He shall be like a tree planted by the rivers of water, that brings forth its fruit in its season, whose leaf also shall not wither; and whatever he does shall prosper."* It is no secret that God blesses those who follow and obey his Word, it is his promise. If we obey him, blessing shall come. Word! I have a friend who says that when he agreed with something he said, "word!" I don't know his name, so I call him Word. He always responds with, "word!"

What is this promise God has made for those who obey his word? Every New Year, my wife and I read these scriptures, God's promises of blessings and prosperity. Deuteronomy 28:1-15 (NKJV) says, *"Now it shall come to pass, if you diligently obey the voice of the Lord your God, to observe carefully all His commandments which I command you today, that the Lord your God will set you high above all nations of the earth. And all these blessings shall come upon you and overtake you, because you obey the voice of the Lord your God: Blessed shall you be in the city and blessed shall you be in the country. Blessed shall be the fruit of your body, the produce of your ground and the increase of your herds, the increase of your cattle and the offspring of your flocks. Blessed shall be your basket and your kneading bowl. Blessed shall you be when you come in and blessed shall you be when you go out. The Lord will cause your enemies who rise against you to be defeated before your face; they shall come out against you one way and flee before you seven ways. The Lord will command the blessing on you in your storehouses and in all to which you set your hand, and He will bless you in the land which the Lord your God is giving you. The Lord will establish you as a holy people to Himself, just as He has sworn to you, if you keep the commandments of the Lord your God and walk in His ways. Then all peoples of the earth shall see that you are called by the name of the Lord, and they shall be afraid of you. And the Lord will grant you plenty of goods, in the fruit of your body, in the increase of your livestock, and in the*

Know Well (Wealth) Your Flocks and Herds

produce of your ground, in the land of which the Lord swore to your fathers to give you. The Lord will open to you His good treasure, the heavens, to give the rain to your land in its season, and to bless all the work of your hand. You shall lend to many nations, but you shall not borrow. And the Lord will make you the head and not the tail; you shall be above only, and not be beneath, if you heed the commandments of the Lord your God, which I command you today, and are careful to observe them. So, you shall not turn aside from any of the words which I command you this day, to the right or the left, to go after other gods to serve them."

Prosperity does not mean only financial wealth, but also a better position in all areas of our life. That is why we enjoy reading Deuteronomy 28:1-15, it's God's promise to prosper and set us up in all areas of our lives. About eight times, the Lord asked us to comply with his commandments and you shall be blessed. Now of those eight times, four uses the word "obey." The other terms used were; "walk in His ways," "observe carefully," "heed," and "do not turn aside to the left or right." With that, He makes about twenty-one promises that bless and prospers those who are obedient. Actually, I think there are a lot more promises than the twenty-one mentioned in the above passage. The scripture says, *"And the Lord will grant you plenty of goods."* How many goods are there in plenty? I don't know, but I guess there are more than twenty-one. Plenty is defined as abundance; as much as can be required. I don't know about you, but I can require much. But what is even greater than plenty of goods, *"just as He has sworn to you."* God has "sworn" it to us. When I was an agent on the court room stand, I would swear (solemn affirmation to God) to tell the truth. If I did not, I could have been convicted of perjury. God cannot perjure himself because God cannot lie. God promised blessing and prosperity to those who obey him. How simple is that? I know, I know, Brother Bubba has been living for God for 40 years and he is poorer than the church mouse. I don't know Bro. Bubba, but I would say God's word is infallible, not so much man's life. Showing up to church every Sunday doesn't mean that you are obedient. Look, some people show up for church because that's the only place they can wear all those fancy-flavorful-forgettable outfits and others because they got no other place to be. Some show up just to hear the pastor preach so that they can disagree with the message. To wreak havoc upon the church, you devil. Some show up to share their suffering. Look how I suffer to be here like Christ suffered. Some say I could be elsewhere, but I suffer to be in church. Well, long as I am on suffering, let me say, this suffering spirit has to go. Many Christians believe in the suffering mode of living for God. That too much wealth is not Christ-like. That we should give all we have so that our families live on the brink of poverty. That God will bless us, despite the choices we make to squander or misuse the prosperity he has given us. Listen my friend, one day, we will be held accountable for all the talents we have been given, including our wealth. Sorry, I digressed. How refreshing if someone showed up to church because they loved Jesus.

"Beloved, I pray that you may prosper in all things and be in health, just as your soul prospers." 3 John 1:2(NKJV)

When we lived in the Chicago, Il. area, we shared God's Word with a group from our church. I was about forty years old and we had a nice two-story house. A young man from the group who was in his twenties did not have a nice job nor home. Our home was valued at about $120K and his house was about $50K (on a good day). He was rather offended that we lived so well and were not struggling like he and his family. My wife answered his offense by telling him that if we had what he had, after having worked many more years and made more money, then there would be something wrong with us. Because I had been working for the Federal Government for almost twenty years, God had prospered us. Remember, God prospers up, not down.

During a five and half year period, we had gone from mortgage and credit card consumer debt to paying cash for our home. All without the use of a ski mask and gun. *And you shall remember the Lord your God, for it is He who gives you power to get wealth, that He may establish His covenant which He swore to your fathers, as it is this day."* Deuteronomy 8:18 (NKJV). We were averaging about $90,000 a year in salary. It was not like we did not have money coming in every month. God allowed us to get wealth. You see God kept his part of his promises. We were and are tithers. We were living godly lives. We were not stealing, lying or committing murder. We did not have flat screens televisions, did not take cruises to the Caribbean or drive new cars. We were not wearing those fancy-flavorful-forgettable outfits. We were trying to live, day to day. We had sufficient pay coming in every two weeks, so what happened? Wisdom, or the lack thereof.

After obtaining wealth, the book of Proverbs says you keep wealth and riches by using wisdom. Proverbs 8:17 (RSV) says *"I love those who love me, and those who seek me diligently find me,"* and that wisdom, *"endowing with wealth those who love me, and filling their treasuries,"*(Proverbs 8:21(RSV)).

"A slothful man will not catch his prey, but the diligent man will get precious wealth," (Proverbs 12:27(RSV)).

"Wealth hastily gotten will dwindle, but he who gathers little by little will increase it," (Proverbs 13:11(RSV)).

"A good man leaves an inheritance to his children's children, but the sinner's wealth is laid up for the righteous," (Proverbs 13:22(RSV)).

"Every man also to whom God has given wealth and possessions and power to enjoy them, and to accept his lot and find enjoyment in his toil—this is the gift of God (Ecclesiastes 5:19(RSV)).

We were never in danger of filing bankruptcy, but just living above our means and going into a financial hole. I saw an article on an actor by the name of David Adkins, who has had a rather successful career. He has had parts in several movies and made millions of dollars. He is a very successful comedian and a nice guy. He gives money to help many people in need and reportedly is a very nice tipper. However, in 2009, he was placed in the Top 10 of the worst tax debtors for the state of California owing the state $2.5 million in personal income tax. On December 11, 2009, he filed for Chapter 7 Bankruptcy. In February 2010, Adkins reportedly put up his 2.5 acres hilltop home for sale to ease his tax burdens. Adkins, then filed a second bankruptcy in April 2013, saying that he owed a debt of approximately $11 million. He indicated that $8 million of the $11 million, was owed money in back taxes. Also, the one time, HBO favorite supposedly claimed that he only earns $16,000 per month and owns $131,000 in assets.

If you are a "Googler" and have already looked up Adkins and found out that he was born in Easton, Maryland to Carolyn A. Sisk, moved to Columbia, Maryland with his family and attended Dartmouth College and Juilliard School, where he met and married Laura Linney. That his many acting roles included the play *Thoreau, or, Return to Walden*. If you discovered that information, that's the wrong David Adkins. This David Adkins stage name is "Sinbad." In an article by the Huffpost Celebrity, "Sinbad Broke: Comedian Files for Second Bankruptcy, Sinbad stated "I spent money, and I kept thinking, 'I get one more movie and I'll wipe these bills out,' but that movie never came," he said. "That black pride, I said, 'Man, I'm going to hang in there, I'm going to pay these bills.' So, you owe a million dollars. I can pay that. OK, fines, fees, now you owe two and a half million. 'But I didn't do nothin'!' Now you owe four million." Updated May 20, 2013, Sinbad told Oprah that his current money troubles were not a result of an extravagant lifestyle. "I didn't buy Bentleys. I didn't live large. I invested in me. I invested in a lot of other people. I would not change it; I would not go back," he said. Sinbad said all the money went into paying for equipment, facilities and salaries for his company. When it was pointed out that some people claimed Sinbad was living the stereotype of black entertainers who waste money on cars, clothes and bling once they find success, the comedian said that couldn't be further from his lifestyle.

Dave Ramsey says that your greatest wealth builder, is your income. The greatest threat to our wealth is our neglect to be attentive and our choices and the wisdom or lack thereof, in those choices. From the book of Proverbs, here are some of the scriptures relating to us losing wealth, keeping us impoverished:

A rich man's wealth is his strong city; the poverty of the poor is their ruin. Proverbs 10:15(RSV)

Poverty and disgrace come to him who ignores instruction, but he who heeds reproof is honored. Proverbs 13:18(RSV)

Love not sleep, lest you come to poverty; open your eyes, and you will have plenty of bread. Proverbs 20:13(RSV)

He who tills his land will have plenty of bread, but he who follows worthless pursuits will have plenty of poverty. Proverbs 28:19(RSV)

He who loves pleasure will be a poor man; he who loves wine and oil will not be rich. Proverbs 21:16-17(RSV)

The above scriptures are some of the reasons we don't keep our wealth and lose our prosperity. These scriptures warn us not to be sluggards, drunkards, slackers, pursue worthless adventures, lovers of stuff, slothful, idle or inattentive. In today's society, the current economy, drug and alcohol use, lack of education, gambling and other addictions, natural disasters and large medical expenses all have a strong relationship to the loss of wealth. Let's go back to something I said previously about our financial choices. We don't make choices about the current poor economy, natural disasters, death, unexpected expenses, loss of a job and large medical expenses. However, we make choices to be sluggards, drunkards, slackers, pursue worthless adventures, lovers of stuff, slothful, idle or inattentive of our finances. In plain English, we make choices concerning our living above our pay, spending beyond our means, home and car expenses, bad money advice and even criminal acts. These choices have caused many people to file bankruptcy, become homeless, criminal, starve, and even die. The loss and removal of wealth often leaves people's lives in disarray and makes it difficult for them to maintain proper relationships with God.

Bestselling author, speaker, media contributor, Thomas C. Corley, wrote a book called "Rich Habits." On his website, "richhabits.net" he wrote an article titled, "Wealth and Poverty are Caused by Parenting and Habits." Corley spent five years studying the daily activities of 233 rich people and 128 poor people and discovered there was an immense difference between the habits of the rich and the poor. In his article, he listed some of the habits that will make you rich and some that will keep you poor (or make you poor if you are rich).

The Ten Keystone Rich Habits That Will Make You Rich:

1. Wealthy individuals have eliminated most of their bad daily failure habits and replaced them with good daily success habits
2. Wealthy individuals set daily, monthly, annual and long-term goals. They understand the difference between a wish and a goal.
3. Wealthy individuals engage in 30 minutes a day of daily career-related reading.
4. Wealthy people are healthy people. They exercise aerobically 30 minutes a day, four days a week and stay below their "caloric threshold" (This is the number of calories consumed each day that will neither make you gain weight nor lose weight). For men this ranges from 2,000 calories a day to 2,600 calories a day. For women this ranges from 1,500 calories a day to 2,100 calories a day.
5. Wealthy individuals manage their relationships every day. Strong relationships are the currency of the wealthy. They employ certain strategies to grow their relationships such as: "The Hello Call", "The Happy Birthday Call" and "The Life Event Call". They use a specific strategy to help them increase their Rich Relationships and eliminate their Poverty Relationships.
6. Wealthy individuals live each day in moderation. They eat in moderation, spend in moderation, work in moderation and play in moderation.
7. Wealthy individuals complete at least 70% of the tasks on their daily "to do" list.
8. Wealthy individuals engage in "Rich Thinking". They are upbeat, positive and focused on achievement.
9. Wealthy individuals save a minimum of 10-20% of their income and live off of the remaining 80-90%.
10. Wealthy individuals control their thoughts and emotions, every day.

Poverty Habits That Are Keeping You Poor

- You watch more than one hour of T.V. a day.
- You spend more than an hour a day on recreational Internet use (Facebook, Twitter etc.)
- You eat more than 300 junk food calories a day.
- You drink more than two glasses of beer, wine or hard alcohol a night.
- You drink more than 12 ounces of non-diet soda a day.
- You don't exercise aerobically a minimum of 30 minutes a day, four days a week.
- Your relationships are on an "as needed" basis. You only reach out to your friends to socialize or when you have problems and need their help. You don't call them just to say hello, happy birthday or to congratulate them or console them when something happens in their lives. In other words, you ignore them unless you need them for something.
- Procrastination is the rule rather than the exception. You don't maintain a daily "to do" list, or if you do, you don't accomplish 70% or more of your daily "to do" list each day.
- You devote very little time to your career beyond working. You do not read a minimum of 30 minutes a day of career-related reading material.
- You do not network or volunteer a minimum of 5 hours a month.
- You do the bare minimum at work. You have "it's not in my job description" syndrome.
- You talk too much and don't listen enough. You violate the "5 to 1 Rule" (Listening for 5 minutes for every 1 minute of talking).
- Oftentimes, you are putting your foot in your mouth and saying inappropriate things.

- You are not generous with your time or money with respect to your relationships.
- You are a spender and not a saver. You don't save 10% of your net income every month. You violate the "90 % Rule" (Pay yourself first 10% of your net pay and live off of the remaining 90% of your net pay).
- You spend more than you earn and your debt is overwhelming you.
- You don't control your thoughts and emotions on a daily basis. You lose your temper too often and belittle others too much.
- You think a wish is a goal. Goals require a specific physical activity, otherwise they are just wishes, and wishes don't come true.

Friend, it hurts me to say (well write) this, but a preacher friend of mine told me, "some Christians use their religion as an excuse to be sloppy in their finances." My name is Ted and I agree with what he said. Many Christians look into the Word of God and see a suffering Christ. They believe that God desires that we (Christians) should live a life without comforts. How appalling that the Pastor should drive a nice luxury car. Like Christ, we should live only on faith, for every one of our needs and anything outside of that is not trusting and faithlessness. We had a sister in Christ who assisted my wife and I with our Financial Peace University class at our church. We tried several times to get her to do a budget and start an emergency fund. She initially looked at us like we had horns growing out of our heads. She thought it was near blasphemy to suggest that we would try take control of God's money with a budget. She was greatly opposed to an emergency fund, claiming that it removes faith in God. She continued in her debt, living from paycheck to paycheck. I don't know if she spent a lot of time watching TV, drank more than 300 calories of soft drinks, didn't exercise 30 minutes a day or didn't know the difference between a goal and a wish or not. I know her mind and spirit were locked into a certain path and she, by faith, was not going to alter it. Why do we need God if we have budgets? Why do we need God if we have emergency funds? Why do we need God if we have savings? Get ready for it, because it all belongs to God and we are his managers. As managers, we need to do budgets, have emergency funds and savings. We do similar things for our jobs, why wouldn't we do more for our God?

In an article title "Wealth and religion" from Wikipedia, the free encyclopedia, it reported "According to a study from 2015, Christians hold the largest amount of wealth (55% of the total world wealth), followed by Muslims (5.8%), Hindus (3.3%) and Jewish (1.1%). According to the same study it was found that adherents under the classification Irreligion or other religions hold about 34.8% of the total global wealth." The article discussed factors (education, children, labor rates and the nations EDP) other than religion that affected the outcome of the study. Despite the mention of these other than religious factors, it is difficult to look beyond the fact that over 50% of the world's wealth is in the hands of Christians. Now, I believe and am sure the Bible indicates that obedience is a major key to prosperity. Someone said prosperity is the results of obedience. My name is Ted and I agree with what he said.

Finally, as I have previously stated, I feel strongly that obedience to God is a path to wealth and prosperity. It is God's promise to those who obey him. Just like when my mother would say, "y'all clean this yard and I will give y'all a nickel (that has to be a violation of some child labor laws)." It was her promise, her word and I trusted her. That nickel was spent before it even hit my grubby little hand. Two scriptures always come to my mind when I think about living a successful life for God: Ecclesiastes 12:13 (NKJV) *Let us hear the conclusion of the whole matter: Fear God and keep*

His commandments, for this is man's all. And Acts 10:34-35 (NKJV) Then Peter opened his mouth and said: "In truth I perceive that God shows no partiality. 35 But in every nation, whoever fears Him and works righteousness is accepted by Him. Where these scriptures say "fear," I see reverence, faith, belief and/or trust in God. Without getting too churchy, I simply feel in my spirit, trust and obey God. His promises of wealth and prosperity will come, sometimes spiritually and sometimes physically. Then of course, what we do with our finances, results in our level of wealth and prosperity.

Rabbi Daniel Lapin in his book, "Thou Shall Prosper," copyright 2010 and published by John Wiley and Sons Inc., Hoboken, NJ, opines that trust is needed for a money system to be successful. "That without some sort of invisible network of trust throughout the communal system, there can be no money." I trust that when I take a dollar to the dollar store, they will give me something, like a bag of pork rinds, popcorn, or any other item for that dollar. I take money to Wal Mart and trust they will exchange some merchandise at a value to the money. Ain't that funny, we trust in this money system or we wouldn't work for it. But the money we get paid has "In God We Trust" on it. Are we trusting God when it's our overspending, broke and irresponsible government that makes the money? I think I will take my chances and trust God. For me, his promises of prosperity for obedience has been worth that chance.

Additionally, in the previous chapter on Stewardship, we talked about how Moses confronted Pharaoh in Exodus, remember what Moses said to Pharaoh, "no!" You want prosperity? Learn to say no, no to wants, desires, convenience and pleasures. Like it says in Proverbs 12:16-21 (RSV) *"He who loves pleasure will be a poor man; he who loves wine and oil will not be rich."* You want prosperity? Say no to the Joneses, to the banks, to the credit card companies, to tv commercials and most likely, to family. After you say no, then the door to prosperity will open.

REFLECTIONS

Do you believe that God has a life of prosperity for you?

Can you see your income as your greatest wealth builder?

Proverbs says prosperity is the reward of the righteous, how is that true with your finances?

Giving

2 Corinthians 9:6-7(NASB) *Now this I say, he who sows sparingly will also reap sparingly, and he who sows bountifully will also reap bountifully. Each one must do just as he has purposed in his heart, not grudgingly or under compulsion, for God loves a cheerful giver.*

My Momma was a giver. Now she raised seven children with very limited help. No not only did we not have much, at times we basically had nothing. Despite our financially challenged situation, it seemed that my momma always had something to give to a relative, friend or neighbor. I did not understand why she would help someone else when we ourselves were in extreme dire need. I found it difficult to grasp, especially when she gave away food. Maybe I was just a greedy little kid, but I remember other kids laughing at me because they could count my ribs, I was so skinny. I thought, give away anything, except the food. Ask anyone who has eaten my mother's cooking and they will say that she was a great cook, which was true. She believed that there was healing in her cooking because people were healed after eating her food. This made her feel blessed. When my mother gave stuff away, particularly food, she not only considered it to be a blessing to the person who received it, she believed her giving would also be a blessing to her. When I look back over our lives, especially the times we left all our stuff behind in Texas and moved to Ohio (twice), we somehow received more and better stuff. The last time we left Texas, we moved from a two-bedroom wooden shack into a five-bedroom brick house. It seems like in no time, our house was full of furniture. Now understand, there were no moving trucks or cars to load up. We travelled from Texas to Ohio on the dog, the Greyhound bus. We didn't even have suit cases to put our clothes in. Our matching luggage were brown card board boxes. So how did that house get filled with furniture? I just believe that it was a result of a promise from God. It brings tears to my eyes when I look back over those times. I have seen the blessings of God and his promises fulfilled.

Luke 6:38(NKJV), *Give, and it will be given to you: good measure, pressed down, shaken together, and running over will be put into your bosom. For with the same measure that you use, it will be measured back to you."*

I am not trying to tell you anything you haven't already heard or read about giving. However, it does mystify me that with almost fourteen hundred scriptures in the bible pertaining to giving, people would have a problem giving. Starting in the book of Genesis, first chapter God said, "Let there be light" and he gave his Light to the world. Christ gives to us in the last book of the bible, Revelation (22:12(NKJV)), Jesus said *"And behold, I am coming quickly, and My reward is with Me, to give to everyone according to his work."* Jesus is giving us rewards for what we have done and for what we have given.

We are asked to give to God, take care of family and help others. Simple, but somehow, we complicate this simple task. How much should I give God? Should I pay God first or take care of my bills first? Do I just pay a tithe (10%) or a tithe and an offering? If all God wants is a cheerful giver, I just need to be happy with what I give, right? Is it OK to charge my giving to my credit card? Is my giving to family members the same as giving to God? Do I have to give to every person holding a cardboard sign on the street corner? Should I question the person to whom I am giving as to their intentions with the gift? And many more.

I have heard that there are four types of giving: tithes, seed (offering), first fruits and alms. I believe giving the tithe is a simple act of obedience in addition to God's promise of a reward. Malachi 3:10(NKJV), *Bring all the tithes into the storehouse, that there may be food in My house, And try Me now in this," Says the Lord of hosts, "If I will not open for you the windows of heaven and pour out for you such blessing that there will not be room enough to receive it.* The seed offering is planted in the church and ministry with an expectation of a larger harvest. 2Corinthians 9:7-8(NKJV), "*So let each one gives as he purposes in his heart, not grudgingly or of necessity; for God loves a cheerful giver. 8 And God is able to make all grace abound toward you, that you, always having all sufficiency in all things, may have an abundance for every good work."* If the seed offering is planted or given to a worthy cause, God promises great returns. First fruits are given when there is an increase of your income from the previous year. It shows God that you have placed him before money and that you are a grateful steward who trusts him to provide. Proverbs 3:9-10(NKJV) *"Honor the Lord with your possessions, and with the first fruits of all your increase; So your barns will be filled with plenty, And your vats will overflow with new wine."* Once again, we see God's promise of plenty to those who invest into his kingdom. Alms are normally given to people because they have a need. Motivation is sympathy and love and often, the reward is joy. Jesus suggests your alms to be given in private, protecting the dignity of those in crisis. Proverbs

19:17(NKJV), *"He who has pity on the poor lends to the Lord, And He will pay back what he has given."* God even promises a repay for almsgiving.

Well I am going to throw one more type of giving into the mix and that is ungodly giving. Ungodly giving is when we give God's money (like it says in the book of Proverbs) into things like; following worthless pursuits, and spending on pleasurable items like wine and oil. Matthew 25:26 (NKJV) *"But his lord answered and said to him, 'You wicked and lazy servant, you knew that I reap where I have not sown and gather where I have not scattered seed. So you ought to have deposited my money with the bankers, and at my coming I would have received back my own with interest.* 1Timothy 5:8(NKJV), :*But if anyone does not provide for his own, and especially for those of his household, he has denied the faith and is worse than an unbeliever."* Proverbs 21:17(NKJV) *He who loves pleasure will be a poor man; He who loves wine and oil will not be rich.* Proverbs 21:20(KJV) *There is treasures to be desired and oil in the dwelling of the wise; but a foolish man spendeth it up.* Whether it is loving stuff, foolishness, being disobedient, an unbeliever or wickedness, they all add up to ungodly giving or use of God's money. There are no promises from God in those cases, just curses.

Giving to God for me and my wife is simple. After enduring such a difficult financial struggle in the early years of our marriage, we had to trust in God, because we had no one else. We gave thanks to God when we had just enough money to pay bills. Slowly, we were able to get to a place where we began tithing. Then we became tithers. Now, we are tithers plus an offering. It is not only built into our budget, but it is a part of our spiritual DNA. In the fourteenth chapter of Genesis when Abram fought against the four kings who had taken Lot, his nephew, and much property. After defeating them, Abram returned with Lot and the recovered property and Melchizedek, King of Salem, brought out bread and wine;

for he *was* the priest of God Most High. Melchizedek blessed Abram and Abram gave Him a tithe of all he had. In the seventh chapter of the book of Hebrews, event was written again. However, in Hebrews, Abram is called Abraham and that he gave Melchizedek a tithe of all he had. In fact, the tithe is mentioned five times in the first ten verses of the seventh chapter. Then of course, the icing on the cake for my little simple mind was; Malachi 3:8-10 (NKJV) *"Will a man rob God? Yet you have robbed Me! But you say, 'In what way have we robbed You?' In tithes and offerings.* Boom! goes the Word. Look, if I am wrong, I err on the side of giving and not robbing God. My editor says, giving is a choice, a lifestyle, a way of living. God does not need your money." I wonder if I have to pay her for that quote.

Christin Ditchfield, host of "Take It To Heart!" an internationally syndicated radio program, in a message titled "Henry Parsons Crowell, Part Two" said the following:

"As a teenager, Henry Crowell had been inspired by the words of evangelist D.L. Moody: The world has yet to see what God can do with and for and through and in a man, who is fully and wholly consecrated to Him."

"Henry prayed, "Oh God...If You will allow me to make money, to be used for Your service, I'll keep my name out of it. I'll do it so You will get the glory."

In every business decision, Crowell made a point of praying for God's guidance. As the founder of Quaker Oats, he pioneered all kinds of innovations in advertising and product development, quickly becoming one of the most successful businessmen of his time. He had always tithed faithfully, giving ten percent of his income to the Lord's work. As God continued to bless his business ventures, Henry discovered that he could pay all of his bills, save for the future, invest in new opportunities, and still have plenty of money left over. He began to give beyond the tithe and even more of his income, until eventually he was giving away seventy percent of his income – a practice he continued for more than forty years."

It is amazing that Crowell's desire to make money was for God's service and God's glory and not for himself. Tithing and commitment to God does work.

We talked about wealth in the last chapter. Wealth to help the Kingdom of God and your family and also to help others. If it is more blessed to give than to receive, we should all be blessed. We now have a world full of needy people. If we are not careful, our hearts can become hardened to the needs of so many. According to the US Census Bureau, Income and Poverty in the United States: 2014, dated September 2015; In 2014, the official poverty rate was 14.8 percent. There were 46.7 million people in poverty. Neither the poverty rate nor the number of people in poverty were statistically different from the 2013 estimates. If nothing else, this indicates there are a lot of people appearing to need help. Whereas we all need some kind of help, not all are in need of financial help. I know Christians who give to virtually every person they encounter at traffic corners. May God bless them, just be prepared to answer if one day the Lord asks, "What did you do with the wealth I gave you?" God's stewards have proper plans for God's money.

Proverbs 21:26(NKJV), *"He covets greedily all day long, But the righteous gives and does not spare."*

Proverbs 22:9,(NKJV), *"He who has a generous eye will be blessed, For he gives of his bread to the poor."*

Proverbs 28:27(NKJV), *"He who gives to the poor will not lack, But he who hides his eyes will have many curses.*

My friends, I am not saying, not to give to people who

stand on corners, but I am suggesting that you be led of God and have a plan for God's money.

When our oldest son and his wife had their last child, they were going to suffer financially while she was off work during her maternity leave. She was not going to be paid while on maternity leave. God put it our hearts to assist them during their trying time. We made up the difference during her maternity leave for three months. Then our youngest son and his wife had their first child, they were facing the same situation. For about five straight months, we made up the financial difference in our children's budgets. They did not ask us too. We did this, not because we had to, but because we wanted to. We had positioned our finances securely, we were able to provide alms to our children who were in need. Remember 1Timothy 5:8(NKJV), *"But if anyone does not provide for his own, and especially for those of his household, he has denied the faith and is worse than an unbeliever."*

We have also been blessed enough to help our extended families. Not patting ourselves on our backs, but acknowledging that God has blessed us to sometimes be a blessing to others. We share with our students that if your Uncle Frick-N-Frack or Aunt Ju-Ju are always asking you for money and you give (not loan) them the money and they are not part of your budget. Congratulations, you have become their emergency fund. How about this, simply tell them you don't have them or the money in your budget to help them. Our students have said they feel bad telling loved ones that, especially when they have money available in their accounts. It seems to some of them that we are telling them to lie. Look, we are not stingy people, maybe frugal, but I don't think stingy, nor are we liars or would we have our students become liars for a dollar. We have told them they don't have money that is available in their budget for their aunts and uncles. Here's why. As we discussed before, in Dave Ramsey's FPU, he teaches to give every dollar a name in your budget before the check hits the bank. Therefore, before they had even received the dollar, it was named Church, Food, Gas, Electricity, Mortgage, Blow, Moe, and Joe. Proverbs 3:28 (TLB) says, *"Don't withhold repayment of your debts. Don't say "some other time," if you can pay now."* Therefore, you have put it in writing (budget) that you owe every dollar to someone or something and the Bible says to pay those people or things while you have money in your possession to pay them. So, when your cousin "Gimme" shows up and wants you to be their emergency fund, you can honestly tell them the money in your budget has been committed to other debts or payments. We are not saying not to help, rather we are saying if you want to give them money, put cousin Gimme in your budget. Because if you don't add them to your budget and you give to them, they become budget busters. This is why, it is always important to know well the condition of your flock, be attentive to your herds. Give to them you owe, because that is what you're supposed to do. Give to others to help them because you can afford it and it brings joy to your God.

Don't think that we gave money to everyone that asked us. Actually, we helped out some by not giving to them. As stewards, I believe we will have to one day answer for the resources God has put into our hands. Therefore, we must appraise every request with prayer. Knowing our budget (how much funding is available), wise reasoning (ask questions) and agreement (between spouses), should we then only render a decision. Family and relatives have asked us for everything from $2 to $25,000 (what were they smoking?). It might seem kind of ridiculous, but my wife and I have discussed the giving of a couple of dollars. Why? Not because we did not have it, but this person would always come to me after church services and ask for a few dollars. I really didn't think much about it until after about the fifth or sixth time and I mentioned it to my wife, if she had a few dollars to give this person. She and I discussed it and my wife said no. It seemed that this person had also asked her several times and when she said no, this person came to me with the same request. Well not to mention, my wife had a few choice names referring to this person. Of course, a cousin had asked me about a $25 thousand loan. My cousin told me he was involved in a disagreement with a business partner and they were disengaging their union and the $25 K was needed to buyout the partner. I told them I would have to talk to my wife. Of course, I really didn't have to talk to her because I already knew what the answer was, but as I had learned after 30 years with the Federal Government, I was following procedures. It's like looking for a soft place to land as you are walking into your boss's office to ask for a raise after you just received a raise. Cause you know he is going to knock you on your bottom. Yes, we had $25 thousand, but we had just placed it into a six-month investment. After telling my wife their story and she suggested they work out some other arrangements that might involve a longer compensation period or maybe attempt to borrow smaller amounts (like $5K) from more people. I called my cousin back and relayed the suggestions to their dilemma. My cousin then asked for $5K. I told them we didn't have that to give either. A couple years later I saw my cousin and asked about the outcome of that situation. My cousin said they were able to work things out with their partner.

As a wise steward, when we examine requests for funds from our budget, we often discover there is not a need for the money if the person just prioritized their finances or they did not need as much as they had asked. I will tell you this now, if you were to ask us to loan you some money, we will tell you that you have the wrong Banks. Ha-ha, play on our name, never mind. For our family who have called for money, we ask a lot of questions. Some of them want to respond about how we be, "all up in their government (business)." My wife's response is that you called us, we did not call you. People, it is God's money, however, we are the stewards over his money. Guess what, it ain't (Texan talk) like we can hide what we are doing from God with his money. It is your budget to support God's Kingdom, your family and to help others. Remember, giving is to help others, not hurt yourselves.

In 2001, we were living in the Kansas City, Kansas. If you live in the KC area, it is important to spell out whether you live on the K (Kansas) or MO (Missouri) side. We were K's living in Kansas going to church on the MO's side. The church we were attending was in the middle of a desperately needed church building program, since we had no church building. We had sold our church building and over the next several years, had rented spaces in several churches, including one building we called, "The Barn." The church asked for pledges toward the purchase of land and the building of our church. God Blessed our church greatly with a piece of property that exceeded all of our pastor's requirements. That the property sat upon a hill, on a major expressway, was several acres of land, had utilities, road accessible, and was located in KC, MO. The church found and purchased a piece of property that met everything the church was praying for. The miraculous thing about that piece of property was that, it had been available to the church several years earlier without utilities or road accessibility at almost twice the price the church paid for it. We had little to no debt and pledged three thousand dollars toward the new construction. We paid the pledge and on the site of that property is a wonderful three building church. We feel blessed to have participated.

In 2006 we were attending church in Austin, TX. Once again, we were in the mist of a church building program, even though somewhat different. The church we were attending decided to construct an add-on, Sunday school building to our main building. My wife and I again prayed about the amount we should pledge. Now if you and your spouse have

Know Well (Wealth) Your Flocks and Herds

ever prayed about an amount to give, you are familiar with this exchange of statements:

I asked my wife, "Well what did God tell you to pledge?" She responded, "Well, what did he tell you to pledge?" I said, well I am not sure, but we should pledge something. "Like what?" "I don't know," I said. My wife asked, "What do you think God wants us to pledge?" Well, since we couldn't agree on a pledge, we decided not to give a pledge. Instead, we made an offer to give. My wife agreed that was OK. Then she asked, "What are we going to offer to give?" "I don't know," I answered. "What did God tell you to offer to give?" I questioned. "I don't know," she answered. "What did God tell you?" She asked.

Eventually I told her I think our offer to give had a three in it. She said like $3,000, like we had given the other church. I told my wife I think God wants us to stretch ourselves this time. Now mind you, we were about $44,000 in debt at the time. Please, don't try this at home, unless you hear THAT VOICE, the voice of the Almighty God and He tells you the pledge amount while you are standing on top of your kitchen table, in formal attire, at midnight. I said, "no," I think it's more like $30,000. She looked at me like I had just grown an afro. Those of you who know me, know that I am completely bald, except for my eyebrows, mustache and nose hairs. Then she said "OK, if that is what you think God told you." We were in church at the time doing the churchy thing, good old Brother and Sister Banks. What I really wanted to say is I don't know what I should be giving. However, I know this, if it was my decision, I never would have said $30,000. When we got home, there was a different conversation that went on about the amount we were going to offer. And it wasn't churchy. But it was too late, we had already turned in the pledge (offer) card with the amount ($30,000) we were offering to give.

Like I said, $56,000, no, now $86,000 in commercial debt

plus $332,000 in mortgage debt on two homes (one as our primary home and a second one we were attempting to flip). The bottom line is that we sold the flip house and received a check for $28,000. Along with a couple of thousand dollars, we paid off the church pledge. Now, how good is God when he says, "Those that water, shall be watered." In 2011, we received a settlement to a class action law suit against my employer, the Government. The check was about $59,000. In 2012, we sold our primary house and received a check for about $113,000. Later in 2012, just before I retired, I was paid $10,000 because I had saved the Government over $50,000 on the sale of our house. Now here is the bottom line of the bottom line, we paid $160,000 **CASH** for the forclosed house we live in now. Presently, the house is valued over $250K. Is God good or what? Proverbs 11:25(RSV) says, "*A liberal man will be enriched, and one who waters will himself be watered.*"

God is faithful to his Word.

You cannot become the giver you ought to be by remaining the giver you are.

Giving is like life, it is constantly evolving.

So as a good steward, we should know well the condition of our flocks and herds. We should know what we have, to know what we can give. God has allowed us good health, so we can build wealth to give away. In the parable of the Rich Fool (Luke 12:16-21(NKJV):

"Then He (Jesus) spoke a parable to them, saying: "The ground of a certain rich man yielded plentifully. And he thought within himself, saying, 'What shall I do, since I have no room to store my crops?' So he said, 'I will do this: I will pull down my barns and build greater, and there I will store all my crops and my goods. And I will say to my soul, "Soul, you have many goods laid up for many years; take your ease; eat, drink, and be merry."' But God said to him, 'Fool! This night

your soul will be required of you; then whose will those things be which you have provided?' So is he who lays up treasure for himself, and is not rich toward God." The Rich Fool showed his selfishness with his wealth. With no thoughts of helping others, only focusing on himself. He was called "Fool" because a fool is one lacking in sense and wisdom. The rich fool did not get that he was all about himself and his needs and desires. The wise get that it is not about them, but about taking care of family and others.

I pointed out earlier, there are always people in need and even more who will take your money if you offer it. Be aware of your emotion when faced with the opportunity to give. I get it, those little puppy dogs need warm homes to live in; those people need wells dug in order to have fresh water to save lives; to give food to the children who are dying of starvation, funds for the building of a hospital; offering for the reverend's new car; money for the pastor's new brown shoes; etc. I once was in church and the pastor instructed the ushers to lock the church doors. He was going to take up an offering because the church needed new ceiling fans, and no one was going to leave until the amount needed had been collected. Now I was a visitor in that church that Sunday. Do you think I ever went back to that church? You are right, I didn't. We can all recall numerous occasions where people have asked for our money in ways we would consider, questionable. Please don't let those instances deter you from giving to meet a godly need. Pray about it, research it out, talk it out, etc., do whatever you have to do, but be aware of emotions, especially guilt, sometime used by requesters. Know that we often bring guilt giving upon ourselves. If we helped one relative, we felt guilty if we didn't give to another relative's request for help, even though their situations might have been the same. If we give to one indigent person on a corner, we guilt ourselves into giving to the next one and the next one...until we are guilted into giving to every person on the corner.

Friend of mine, God wants us to be a cheerful giver, not a guilty giver. I don't believe God wants us to dodge certain street corners because of the people there, desiring money, or ducking relatives because of their perceived need. God wants us to give bountifully, not because he needs the money back. He wants us to reap bountifully from his warehouse. Amazon just built an 855,000 square feet warehouse in Texas, that is almost 20 acres. Now that's big, even in Texas. In college, I played football in a blimp hangar in Akron, OH. It was just over 8 acres of floor space an area larger than 8 football fields side-by-side, 22 stories high. While playing the game, it rained on the teams due to the condensation that builds up inside of the hangar. The Boeing Everett Factory in Everett, Washington is over 98 acres and is the world's largest warehouse. I said all of that just to say this, now just think how large God's warehouse must be. He desires to "open for you the windows of heaven and pour out for you *such* blessing that *there will* not *be room* enough *to receive it.*" I don't know exactly what a poured-out blessing might be from a divine warehouse, but if he is willing to give me a blessing for what I have given, I am willing to receive a blessing gladly.

Brad Formsma is the author of "*I Like Giving: The Transforming Power of a Generous Life*" and the creator of the web site "ilikegiving.com." I like giving is a movement which Formsma hopes to inspire people to live generously. By giving into peoples' lives, Formsma tells how lives have changed, including the lives of the givers. In one of his stories, he tells how a woman lost her husband and a child in a house fire. He suggested that we don't say to people "Hey if you need anything, let me know." Formsma said this puts an added burden on the person. He says, "The best thing to do is if you see a need, give it. If you can do something large, give large, but if you can only do a little, give a little." In any local church, there are people with needs. Local churches have limited financial means to help not only their members, but also non-members. Our church, like other churches normally have benevolent funds and food pantries to help the needy, but as always, the funds and food are limited. But, if you desire to help a family, go to any of these churches and ask the pastor if you can give to a family in need. That pastor will have no shortage of names.

According to Dave Ramsey, in a blog article "Five Traits of Fulfilled People," one of the traits is that the fulfilled are givers. "The most fulfilled people are the most generous. After all, giving is the most fun you can have with money! They feel so blessed that they're compelled to give to others." God loves a cheerful giver and cheerful givers feel fulfilled. Giving does provides me a unique feeling of gratitude, because I am grateful to God to be able to help give. Rachel Cruze (Dave's daughter) in her book, 'Love Your Life, Not Theirs,' she writes "Generosity isn't an event or a simple act of giving. Generosity is a lifestyle that changes hearts and minds as it blesses everyone involved. I have learned over the years that giving is the most fun you can have with money. I have to say, I am hooked." Being hooked into God's Will is not only a blessing to those who receive, but also fulfilling to those who give.

Finally, you have probably heard it said, "We are closest to God when we give." The scripture says, "For God so loved the world, He gave..." We then should give, especially when we have it in our means. Our suggestions on giving were not to get your fix or high on giving, because the focus in on you. Again, appraise your giving with some seeking or prayer to God's direction. Don't appraise to support your justification of your giving. There are only a few greater moments in life than an opportunity of maximum giving. Meeting someone's life need through God's will and his timing. Not that you are giving some maximum amount of money, but that you are giving the amount according to God's Will to meet the need in that person's life. Another thing, your maximum giving might not be money. Sometimes people think that they need money, when what they needed was the Word, wisdom, help or a hug. It is a great blessing to have money, but even greater when those finances are wisely channeled through their hands to affect the lives of others. We are wise to understand the use of those finances in our lives. Finances do not make you what you are, they reveal what you are. It is a great thing when we are obedient to that still voice concerning our giving. When we give by the Spirit's direction, I believe we position ourselves to receive God's Blessings. I said earlier my grandmother use to tell me, "If you look for boogy-bears, you will find one behind every bush." If you look for opportunities to give, you will find one behind every door. If you look to God for opportunities to give, you will find one behind every bush and will have an opportunity to change a person's life.

This was not a book about a rags to riches story. Even though our financial adviser said my pension equates us to be a millionaire. I asked her, "what part?" We do not feel like millionaires, nor do we live like millionaires. Nor was this book about how to become rich. Even though we have more than enough wisdom to share from our experience. This book was a lot of little things which came together for the success of our family, orchestrated by God. This book was our experience with our finances, based on our decisions. Speaking of decisions, I heard a preacher say, "Good decisions, good life, bad decisions, bad life." It is the same with our finances, good decisions, good finances, bad decisions, bad finances. You heard about our bad decisions and hopefully you saw some of our better decisions. Like to take a finance course to better our understanding of the financial spectrum of this world. After we completed the course, we had a meeting with each other on what we wanted to accomplish with our finances.

Know Well (Wealth) Your Flocks and Herds

We then constructed a budget, agreed to it and began to live with it. Things were tight at first, no, more like constriction with no wiggle room. My wife made sure of that. On one occasion she was doling out my portion of gas money for my car and I questioned if it was enough for me to make it back and forth to work. I asked her what I would do if I ran out of gas. She said call her and she would come and get me. I was hoping for more cash. After we paid off a few small bills, the constriction lessened and we began to feel confident that we could better our financial standing. After a year of working our program, we began to believe that we could get out of debt before we reached our golden years. After two years, we were decreasing our debt so fast, we started looking at target dates when we were going to be debt free. We became debt free sooner than the dates we set. We were free! No more slavery!

One last thing, before we began making any decisions, we had to know. Know what? We had to know the condition of our flocks and herds. We couldn't have made a financial decision if we did not know the state of our finances. We couldn't have constructed a budget without knowing how much debt we had, how much money we had and how much money we had coming in. Once we knew the status of our finances and also God's money, we acknowledged that we were stewards and not the owners. We began to work our budget plan until we were both satisfied with the direction of our finances. We both had to humble ourselves and give up control of our portion of the money for the sake of a family victory over debt. We had to know how to say no. If you do not have the finances to do it, then don't. Understand, some of us do not want to appear cheap, tight, poor, stingy, selfish, tightwad or heaven forbid you get called, Scrooge. So let me be your financial adviser. When someone asks you to spend money that is not in your budget, I want you to say, "I would love to do what you have asked me, however, my financial adviser instructed me to hold off on such financial endeavors until he be consulted." Or just say no. Another thing that you must know is this, you must know that you can do this. The only thing special about me and my wife is that Christ reigns in our lives. If we can do this, know that you can do likewise or even do better. Everybody has a story. You just read ours. Now go out and make your own story.

Be blessed in Jesus' Name

REFLECTIONS

Do you give of your time or money to charitable organizations?

Do you give to fulfill your needs or to fulfill the needs of thers?

Why is it important to give?

Consultation Stories

Family #1. This first story is rather disheartening. This family, Adam and Ava, who attended our church, came to by way of a financial request for help. However, before they were referred to us, we knew them. Adam was a participant who attended our church, came to us for consultation. He had asked for help to move from their apartment to another apartment. I went over to help and saw that they were not ready to be moved. Maybe they had 20% of their goods packed and ready to go. I also learned that they were not just moving, but that they were being evicted. Subsequently, I found out that Adam and Ava had not paid their rent in about six months. I could see that they needed help.

When Adam and Ava came in to consult with us, they were about $16K in debt. The church had given them a minivan to help their situation a year prior. They had gotten a title loan on the van and were operating on payday loans to stay afloat. They had four dependents, one of which was living outside of the home. The couple's combine salaries were $39K a year, that was approximately $1950 per month. Their expenses were about $3063 per month. This put them about $1100 a month in the hole.

Adam and Ava consulted with us a second time about four years after their initial consultation. They had also taken the FPU class at our church. They said before they had the consultations and the class, they had no outlook on their incoming money, nor were they paying their bills. Adam said they had no written budget, Ava said they had no financial direction and they were using pay day loans to augment their money woes. She teared up and commented the pay day loan places were taking money out of their bank accounts. After the consultations, Ava mentioned that she had just started working a new job and was not sure how much money she was earning. She said once she began budgeting, she was able to help their finances tremendously. Adam began working a second job and they began to experience more money in their finances. However, she felt that her husband was sacrificing church by working the second job. She considered their life to be a unique situation, saying as they were climbing up the hill (out of debt), they (always) got bumped back down. For example, she received a pay raise on her job and at the same time, her employer raised the premium on her health insurance. She was literally working for about $300 a month. She said she then suffered a life-threatening illness that put them into a bigger financial hole. Ava claimed it was always something, they knew that something bad is going to happen to them. The couple mentioned that they had a large un-paid electrical bill. They explained they were receiving $650 a month electrical bills and decided not to pay them. At this point, the bills totaled $5,000.

Adam and Ava asserted they have been using a written budget method to better their finances. They stated that they were evicted from their previous residence and had all their household items placed on their front yard. And according to Ava, "it never rains in Austin in the summertime," except for that day and they lost most of everything that they owned. She had been searching the internet and has been able to find free stuff, including household furniture. She said the stuff they have been receiving is better than the stuff they lost. They both said they are better off today than they had been in the past. They are now paying their bills and are current on most everything. They stated they are paying on $1400 of the $5K electrical bill, the remainder was paid by a local government agency. Ava said Adam is a hustler and has brought more money into their finances and she had found further assistance for the family by obtaining food from local food pantries. When asked what their general advice for anyone who was in a similar financial situation, he said first, he would tell them to stop and pray for "an overflow (more than what you needed)." She advised that the person should set priorities, list their debts, draw a line where the money runs out and don't pay those below the line. She further advised that one should have a written budget and stay on the baby steps set forth by Dave Ramsey. This family was recently evicted from their resident and texted me to borrow money regarding their financial woes.

Family #2. The next family was a husband and wife, Bill and Betty, with a small child and a teenager. They are faithful church members and participants in several ministries. Betty was desperately wanting a financial consultation; however, Bill was reluctant to discuss their finances. During consultation, she was emotional, and he was matter-of-fact. Eventually, he humbled himself to share their situation with us. Their combined salaries were $66,344 annually, about $4,580 a month. Their house was not paid for. They had two car loans with monthly payments of $643. They did not receive a tax refund from the previous year, instead had to pay about $5000 to the Internal Revenue Service (IRS). He was nearing retirement with his government job and wanted to get out of debt so that eventually, they could initiate and support a foreign ministry. Their expenses were about $5,845 per month. This put them about $1,255 a month in the hole. Their debt was about $50,000.

About a year later, the couple was interviewed and reported the overall condition of their finances since their consultation. Bill and Betty said prior to the consultation they operated on week to week, paycheck to paycheck financial basis. Due to their funding shortages, they had to depend upon their credit cards to cover those shortages in their finances. They remembered their five credit cards being maxed out at $20K and of course spoke fondly (not) of the $500 a month time-share fee they had to pay. The two described their budget method as making minimum payments on their bills and credit cards. They reportedly made some traction at times but the "revolving door"(some unexpected financial expense) would always come up. Since the consultation, their finances have changed for the better. The two cited they were not as stressed or burdened over financial issues and they were no longer having to dog paddle to stay afloat. They stated their finances were now more balanced. Offering they had sold their house, paid off their credit cards (totaling about $40,000). They were forced to down-size and were now renting. They did admit to buying a new car but was using the vehicle to make money by driving for one of the ride-hailing services. Their budget method changed to a written budget. They are using a combination of Dave Ramsey teaching with some of their own modifications. They have not met their financial goals but expect to meet them in about two and a half years. The husband plans on retiring in two years and will add about $2,400 a month to the budget. The husband and wife stated their general advice for anyone who might presently be in their former financial situation is to count the cost (Luke 14:28) and to pray for understanding. They said for the couple, it will take a lot of sacrifice on their parts to be successful. Bill and Betty explained there will be long suffering needed in their efforts. Also, for them not to quit, especially if it looks like you are not getting anywhere. Both suggested to turn off the TV and ignore the advertisements which lured you to buy stuff that you don't need. They said they bought stuff that they did not need, they sold some of it back. Finally, they both suggested that discipline must play a major part in anyone's efforts to get out of debt.

Family #3. This family contained six members, the husband and wife (Cam and Carla), two young adults and two teenagers. The husband, wife and teenagers were faithful members of the church. Just from looking at their submitted financial forms, we suspected that this family was special. The husband had a $3,000 a month gross income, but they had placed the word "unsure" and "???" next to the monthly take home pay. They reported that they had not completed tax filing for 2013 and 2014. They also reported that they were in $55,908.82 of debt. I felt like we would be dealing with extremes with this couple, on one hand they were not sure what they brought home every month but on the other hand, they knew their precise debt, down to the penny. Additionally, the family provided almost two handwritten pages of explanations regarding their finances. Specifically, Carla provided information that they had or were experiencing water disconnection, gas disconnection, cable, internet disconnection and electrical disconnection. Multiple personal loans from family members, toll road billings, medical bills, credit cards, etc, and even payments to a Bad Check Attorney. Cam stated several of his customers owed his company thousands of dollars, which could have gone to helping their finances tremendously. But there were issues with him collecting much of those outstanding debts from his customers.

Cam was an independent general contractor who owned his own business. He was not greatly concerned about their finances because in his mind, he was going to catch up to the debt. Carla however had a different view of their finances and situation. She was frustrated and frightful. She saw no effort of change in her spouse and was very concerned. Their monthly expenses were $4,846. At a $3,000 income, they were $1,846 in the hole many months.

About a year later after several consultations, the couple was interviewed and reported the overall condition of their finances were still in disarray. Carla said that her husband would probably disagree with her analysis of their finances and described the condition of their finances prior to the consultation as chaotic and uncontrolled with no accountability. Cam said their finances were not great and presented the thought that simply, they did not make enough money. The wife stated she budgeted down to the penny while her husband was about damage control with urgent responses when he deemed necessary. She recalled that she set up a budget and her husband's response to it was that it did not matter because they had no money. However, she added that she secretly paid for medical bills and started an emergency fund. The husband agreed that his wife was very orderly, but on the other hand, he is a "take care of things now" kind of person. He said his budget method was out of pocket, paying the worst (most pressing) bills first. When asked if their finances had gotten better or worse since the consultation, the wife retorted, "ten weeks without water, five weeks without gas, they are still cycling." Things had not gotten better. Her perception was that there was no accountability, that her husband made all the financial decisions. Cam said they looked at their budget and he knew there were things he had to pay. He was just trying to take care of the basics but did not have the money. He said it was depressing. Cam decided to change business operations relating to his construction company and move into more profitable areas of his business industry. Hoping that the move would bring more revenue into their budget. He commented that he sought his wife's approval of the move. The couple was next asked about the present budget method they are using. The wife said she has a written budget. The husband did not have a written budget, but that they were talking about it. He acknowledged that they needed a budget, but that they needed more money. They were asked had they met any of their financial goals. The wife said no, but she has a written plan when money becomes available. The husband said no, but he was trying to build up an emergency fund. He was working two jobs, which were going to bring a substantial amount of money into their budget. They were also asked concerning their general advice for anyone who are presently in their financial situation. The wife suggested that the couple share in the financial responsibility. She further suggested that stepping away from your finances possibly gives options for better relations later. She finally suggested a third party that could come along side of a couple and give both equal responsibility in the financial process. The husband echoed the wife's comments by saying that accountability is a good thing. That they should share the financial burden and the use of available monies. He said he has asked for his wife to participate in the financial process, but was unsure if she would do it.

Family #4. This family was also a member of the church however, they came to us for consultation, not asking for financial assistance, but for financial advice. They did not meet the requirement needed to meet with us. One of our requirements to consult with people concerning their finances is that you must have an income. This family had no income due to the husband being laid off because of a medical condition. The husband and wife, Don and Dee, had about $125,200 in home equity and about $77K in savings. They were about $83,800 in debt with a mortgage of $282,737. Their reported monthly expenses were $7,636. They were using their savings, which at one time was several hundred thousand, to cover their monthly expenses. They were concerned about their dwindling savings and asked about using their home equity for a financial relief or possibly filing a personal bankruptcy. Don and Dee took the Dave Ramsey financial class.

Don only was available for the interview and described the overall condition of their finances prior to the consultation as a mess. He said that he and Dee failed to properly save what they needed. The other problem was they were spending their saving with no income coming in. He said they were in dire-straights and worried about losing everything and being out on the streets. One of their biggest problems was that they never kept track of their finances. Their budget type was a pay bills budget. Since the consultation, he assured their finances have changed for the better. He applied for and received social security and permanent disability and his wife has gotten a job. He said they have received a tax refund and he has sold his prize Corvette for $22K to pay off a $20K bank line of credit. He said they have about $24K in debt with $32K in their savings but did not want to pay off the debt and be left with only about $9K in their emergency fund. Presently, he described their budget method they are now using as a hand-written budget, with dual checks from the bank. When asked if they had met their financial goals, he shared that a $25K student loan had been discharged due to his disability. He also shared that within a year, he will be receiving two pensions totaling $770 a month. He said yes, they are meeting their financial goals. He likens their goals to a trip, saying they are traveling, but have not arrived at their destination (yet). He said now, they know where they are going. Don's general advice for anyone who is presently in their former financial situation is to realize that not much is more important than breaking the chains of debt and obtaining financial freedom.

Family #5. Effie, single mother of two, one child at home and the other outside of the home described her financial situation prior to FPU and the consultation as "horrible." She admitted to praying to make it from paycheck to paycheck. She was renting and had no money for anything except for paying bills. Effie had no savings and had no hope of ever buying a house. Her credit card debt was $50k and student loans was $30K. One good thing she had done was to avoid car payments. Her financial method was now a written budget. She said she had listed all her debts and began to pay them off, one by one. After taking the FPU class, my wife became her accountability partner. Effie said her finances have changed for the better. She stated she began to take control of her finances, before FPU, her finances controlled her. She said she now tells her money where to go and considers it to be "empowering." She commented she realized how important it was to have her four walls supported (food, clothing, shelter and utilities, and/or transportation). She also realized she did not have to live according to the FICO score. She began to utilize a written budget and has obtain an emergency fund of $500. When asked about her financial goals, she said as a single mom, her goal was not to have debt, so she paid cash for two cars. Then she did something no one else in her family had done, she bought a house. She recalled needing $7K in her bank account (which she had to borrow from a friend). Now that she is married, she and her husband are working together, and they hope to be out of debt in two years. Her advice for single and married couples is to pay yourself and don't be a slave to the FICO score.

Additional Scriptures

PROSPERITY

"*House and wealth are inherited from fathers, but a prudent wife is from the Lord* (Proverbs 19:14(RSV)

"*Do not toil to acquire wealth; be wise enough to desist,*" (Proverbs 23:4(RSV)).

"*A miserly man hastens after wealth and does not know that want will come upon him,*" (Proverbs 28:22(RSV)).

"*He who loves money will not be satisfied with money; nor he who loves wealth, with gain: this also is vanity,*" (Ecclesiastes 5:10(RSV)).

How long will you lie there, O sluggard? When will you arise from your sleep? A little sleep, a little slumber, a little folding of the hands to rest, and poverty will come upon you like a vagabond, and want like an armed man," Proverbs 6:9-11(RSV)

A slack hand causes poverty, but the hand of the diligent makes rich. Proverbs 10:4(RSV)

Hear, my son, and be wise, and direct your mind in the way. Be not among winebibbers, or among gluttonous eaters of meat; for the drunkard and the glutton will come to poverty, and drowsiness will clothe a man with rags. Proverbs 23:19-21(RSV)

I passed by the field of a sluggard, by the vineyard of a man without sense; and lo, it was all overgrown with thorns; the ground was covered with nettles, and its stone wall was broken down. Then I saw and considered it; I looked and received instruction. A little sleep, a little slumber, a little folding of the hands to rest, and poverty will come upon you like a robber, and want like an armed man. Proverbs 24:30-34(RSV)

Give strong drink to him who is perishing, and wine to those in bitter distress; let them drink and forget their poverty and remember their misery no more. Proverbs 31:6-7(RSV)

Slothfulness casts into a deep sleep, and an idle person will suffer hunger. Proverbs 19:15(RSV)

And of course, one of my favorites; *Know well the condition of your flocks, and give attention to your herds*; Proverbs 27:23(RSV)

NOTES

John Maxwell, Its Just A Thought (Honor Books 1996) 114

Daniel Halper, The Weekly Standard, Over $60,000 in Welfare Spent Per Household in Poverty, Oct. 26, 2012

Scripture from the New King James Version®. Copyright © 1982 by Thomas Nelson.

Sarah Schmalbruch for the Business Insider Jul. 13, 2015, In an article titled "9 rich and famous people who filed for bankruptcy

Natalie Robehmed, Forbes, July 14, 2014, The Vanderbilts: How American Royalty Lost Their Crown Jewels

FDIC study: outrageous overdraft fees Laura Bruce • Bankrate.com

Bloomberg Institute titles "There's a Spot in Hell Reserved for Bank Overdraft Fees" by Ben Steverman 2014-02-27

Wall Street Journal "Banks Fee Bonanza Dries Up" by James Sterngold Sept. 2, 2014

Lee Jenkins, Taking Care of Business, 2001, Moody Publishers

Revised Standard Version (RSV) of the Bible, copyright © 1946, 1952, and 1971 the Division of Christian Education of the National Council of the Churches of Christ in the United States of America.

The Message (MSG) Copyright © 1993, 1994, 1995, 1996, 2000, 2001, 2002 by Eugene H. Peterson;

The Voice (VOICE) The Voice Bible Copyright © 2012 Thomas Nelson, Inc. The Voice™ translation © 2012 Ecclesia Bible Society All rights reserved

Hugh Whelchel is Executive Director of the Institute for Faith, Work & Economics, November 26, 2012

Leadership is Stewardship written by Bill Peel, of The High Calling

21st Century King James Version (KJ21) Copyright © 1994 by Deuel Enterprises, Inc.;

American Standard Version (ASV) Public Domain (Why are modern Bible translations copyrighted?);.;

Amplified Bible, Classic Edition (AMPC) Copyright © 1954, 1958, 1962, 1964, 1965, 1987 by The Lockman Foundation;

Common English Bible (CEB) Copyright © 2011 by Common English Bible;

Complete Jewish Bible (CJB) Copyright © 1998 by David H. Stern. All rights reserved;

Contemporary English Version (CEV) Copyright © 1995 by American Bible Society;

Darby Translation (DARBY) Public Domain (Why are modern Bible translations copyrighted?);

Easy-to-Read Version (ERV) Copyright © 2006 by Bible League International;

Holman Christian Standard Bible (HCSB) Copyright © 1999, 2000, 2002, 2003, 2009 by Holman Bible Publishers, Nashville Tennessee. All rights reserved.;

International Children's Bible (ICB) The Holy Bible, International Children's Bible® Copyright© 1986, 1988, 1999, 2015 by Tommy Nelson™, a division of Thomas Nelson. Used by permission.;

International Standard Version (ISV) Copyright © 1995-2014 by ISV Foundation. sed by permission of Davidson Press, LLC.;

The Message (MSG) Copyright © 1993, 1994, 1995, 1996, 2000, 2001, 2002 by Eugene H. Peterson;

Revised Standard Version (RSV) Revised Standard Version of the Bible, copyright © 1946, 1952, and 1971 the Division of Christian Education of the National Council of the Churches of Christ in the United States of America. Used by permission. All rights reserved.;

Huffpost Celebrity, Sinbad Broke: Comedian Files For Second Bankruptcy (REPORT), 05/20/2013 10:41 am ET | Updated May 20, 2013

Thomas C. Corley, wrote a book called "Rich Habits." Web site "richhabits.net" Article titled "Wealth and Poverty are Caused by Parenting and Habits," April 17, 2014.

US Census Bureau, Income and Poverty in the United States: 2014, dated September 2015, Report Number: P60-252

Christin Ditchfield, host of "Take It To Heart! titled Henry Parsons Crowell, Part Two

Brad Formsma is the author of *"I Like Giving: The Transforming Power of a Generous Life"* 2014 WaterBrook Press and the creator of the web site "ilikegiving.com."

Rachel Cruze, Love Your Life, Not Theirs, Thomas Nelson

U.S. News & World Report article, "5 Rewards of Living a Frugal Lifestyle," by Kassandra Dasent, March 6, 2015 reference.com/pets-animals/much-weight-can-horse-pull

HOUSEHOLD BUDGET

	BUDGETED	ACTUALLY SPENT	DIFFERENCE (+/-)
Monthly Income			
Tithes/Offering	_____		
Check Deductions	_____		
EXPENSES			
Savings	_____	_____	_____
House	_____	_____	_____
Transportation	_____	_____	_____
Food	_____	_____	_____
Utilities (Water, Electric, Gas, Phone, Internet, Cable)	_____	_____	_____
Insurance	_____	_____	_____
Clothing	_____	_____	_____
Medical	_____	_____	_____
Childcare	_____	_____	_____

Entertainment							
Miscellaneous							
Investments							
Sinking Fund							
Debts							
Credit Card							
Credit Card							
Credit Card							
Credit Card							
Student Loans							
Personal Loans							
TOTALS							

RAPID DEBT REPAY

Debt Item	Balance	Payment Made	New Balance
1.			
2.			
3.			
4.			
5.			
6.			
7.			
8.			
9.			
10.			
11.			
12.			

List debts from #1 (Smallest) to #12 (Largest).

Pay off smallest debt first and move the monthly payment amount down to the next debt.

As you pay off debts, move down the accumulated monthly payments made and apply to the next debt until you have no more debt.

www.ingramcontent.com/pod-product-compliance
Lightning Source LLC
Chambersburg PA
CBHW020655220526
45464CB00001B/449